SIMPLE STATISTICS
FOR
LIBRARY AND
INFORMATION

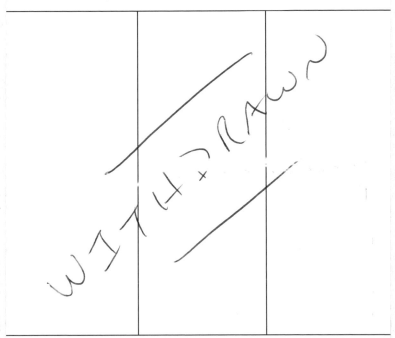

SIMPLE STATISTICS
FOR
LIBRARY AND
INFORMATION
PROFESSIONALS

Peter Stephen

*Senior Lecturer, Department of Library and
Information Studies, Manchester Metropolitan University*

Susan Hornby

*Lecturer, Department of Library and Information Studies,
Manchester Metropolitan University*

LIBRARY ASSOCIATION PUBLISHING
LONDON

Published by
Library Association Publishing
7 Ridgmount Street
London WC1E 7AE

First published 1995

British Library Cataloguing in Publication Data
A catalogue record for this book is available from the British Library

ISBN 1-85604-129-8

Typeset from authors' disks in 10/12pt Times by Library Association Publishing
Printed and made in Great Britain by Bookcraft (Bath) Ltd

Contents

List of figures

Introduction

In their teaching of statistics, the authors have met many students who have dreaded this element in their course, because they were 'no good at maths at school', or because they left school years ago and feel that they have forgotten too much. There will be many in the profession at large who feel the same, who have mainly arts-based backgrounds, and whose library-school courses may not have included a statistics module.

Librarians and other information professionals are nevertheless aware of the need to research, evaluate and measure performance of themselves, their staff and their services. Many librarians now think of themselves as 'managers', and recognize that good management requires good decision-support data. Statistical methods offer a range of meaningful pictures, from simple graphics to the more abstract inferential measures, to support management decisions.

Use of statistical methods requires an understanding not only of techniques but of the reasoning behind them. Maths is not as huge a problem as one may think:

- the higher mathematics involved are reduced to tools and techniques which may be learned;
- the pocket calculator or computer does most of the work;
- most people remember more maths than they imagine, and what is effortlessly used in daily life will take them a long way in statistics.

It is possible to understand statistics in an intuitive way, building mental pictures without necessarily being able to express them in mathematical terms.

This text is written sympathetically. The authors are themselves not outstandingly numerate, and understand the need for a text which does not make the assumptions common to so many others, including some that claim to be 'simple' or 'introductory'. It is written as a tutorial, with a logical and cumulative progression of ideas. It concentrates on understanding what is happening when techniques are applied, and on what conclusions may be fairly drawn from the resulting statistics. Anyone can put figures into a calculator, but what do the answers mean?

In choosing the contents of this book the authors have aimed at practicality and usefulness in the reality of normal working life. No doubt there are statistics which some would have liked to see included. Every teacher has a favourite set! Besides being merely useful, statistics can be a very satisfying skill to acquire, and can lead to an interest in numbers which many people probably never intended to have.

Plan of the book

The book is divided broadly into two areas – descriptive statistical methods and inferential statistics.

Descriptive statistical methods allow us to make quick sense of a set of observations, to be able to make supportable statements such as averages, frequencies, distributions, relationships of frequencies to characteristics such as age groups. In many cases the information gleaned from data can be represented graphically. Descriptive methods provide means of assessing a library's performance in a number of routine areas for which librarians have long collected data. Now it is common for data to be provided as a by-product of an automated housekeeping system, whose programming can potentially offer more information and perform analysis to a degree not practicable using manual methods. This section describes a range of methods of proven usefulness, as well as introducing basic concepts and terminology.

Inferential statistics builds on the basics of descriptive methods and moves into the realms of uncertainty. For example, if we want to know what our readers think of an aspect of the library service it is impracticable to ask every user, so we rely on asking a sample. Do the opinions of the sample accurately reflect the opinions of all registered users?

If sampling is properly conducted the responses of the sample are subject to the laws of probability. These laws and theorems, and a sound mathematical basis, contribute to reducing 'uncertainty' to something that can be measured, and results of a sample may be accepted, or rejected, with a level of confidence based on the strength of probability that such a result could have occurred. These key concepts of confidence and probability are explored and applied in a number of situations.

The text is illustrated by examples and diagrams. Many chapters have further questions for the reader to attempt. In Appendix 1, some of the questions are worked out fully, others more briefly.

The bibliography lists a number of works which the authors have found helpful while struggling to learn the subject themselves. Rowntree's *Statistics without tears* and Paulos' *Innumeracy* are particularly recommended for the clarity with which they make numbers and statistics so accessible.

A final word – no text book can make the learning of statistics 'easy'. The subject is, however, well within the reach of any who are prepared to grapple with something new. We hope that this text will lead you into statistics with confidence and enjoyment.

Symbols and abbreviations used in the text

α	alpha, the measure of risk of making a Type 1 error
CI	confidence interval
CV	cyclical variation
CV	critical value (e.g. Cv_z, CV_t, $CV_{\chi2}$, CV_r)
d	difference (Spearman's correlation)
df	degrees of freedom
E	expected frequency
!	the factorial sign
f	frequency of a value, or the number of cases in a class
H_0	a null hypothesis
H_1	an alternative hypothesis
IQR	the Interquartile Range
L	the lower limit of a class
M	the median
μ	mean of a variable in the population
N	the number of members of a population (in formulas)
n	the number of items in a sample (in formulas)
$n!$	the value of n multiplied by (n-1) $\times$ (n-2) . . .
O	observed frequency
P_N	prices in the current year
P_0	prices in the base year
p	the probability that an event will happen at any trial
p_0	a hypothesized proportion
p_p	a pooled proportion
$p_{\centerdot}$	a sample proportion
Q	Yule's Q, a measure of association between two variables
Q1	the first quartile
Q3	the third quartile
Q_N	quantities in the current year
Q_0	quantities in the base year
q	the probability that an event will not happen at any trial
r	Pearson's product-moment coefficient of correlation

r_s	Spearman's rank-correlation coefficient
SE	standard error of a sampling distribution of means
SND	the Standard Normal Distribution
s	standard deviation of the data in a sample
σ	standard deviation of a variable in a population
$\sigma(\bar{x}_1 - \bar{x}_2)$	the standard error of the sampling distribution of the difference between means
Σ	the summation sign; the sum of all items identified by following characters
t	standardized distribution for use with small samples of quantitative data
U	the upper limit of a class
X	the horizontal axis of a graph
x	values of the variable being investigated
$\bar{x}$	mean of the data in a sample
$\bar{x}_g$	mean of the data in a sample, grouped data
$\dot{x}$	the midpoint of a class of grouped data
χ^2	chi-square, a measure of association between two variables
Y	the vertical axis of a graph
y	values of the variable measured on the Y axis
y'	y prime: the value of y where a value of x strikes the regression line
z	standardized value represented by the Standard Normal Distribution, for large samples of quantitative data

Part 1
Welcome to statistics

Chapter 1
Why bother with statistics?

Summary

At the end of this chapter you should understand the use and abuse of statistics. You should understand its scope, limitations and use in library and information science.

'There are lies, there are damned lies and there are statistics'. This phrase has been quoted on many occasions and you may agree with it, observing the way that some statistics are presented on TV and in the national press. Nevertheless, perhaps you would agree more with H. G. Wells' comment that 'Statistical thinking will one day be as necessary for efficient citizenship as the ability to read and write'.

It is suggested that that day has arrived. Many people who would feel embarrassed and mortified to admit to illiteracy are quite happy to exclaim 'I'm no good at maths'. Being 'no good at maths' nowadays leaves you open to being duped by any statistical charlatan, those that 'use statistics as a drunk uses a lamp-post; more for support than illumination'. It is hoped that this book will enable you to be aware of the more outrageous uses of statistics and to be able to counter spurious arguments.

If you can understand the methods used to collect and to analyse the data you are less likely to be confused by the 'damned lies'. In addition, statistical methods used correctly can give managers and information scientists a good source of sound arguments to support decisions and/or appeals for funds.

Today we are surrounded by statistical data. We need to understand how the data is collected, what methods have been used in its analysis and, most importantly, whether the interpretation is correct.

Many people view statistical research as a pure science. If you think about statistical research it has more than a slightly creative element in it. There are three main stages :

1   You decide on what is going to be your research project and collect the data. This is a creative process.

2   You analyse the data. This is the 'scientific', sometimes called 'number crunching', part of the process.

3   You interpret the data. This is the most creative part of any research process.

To understand fully this creative process we only have to listen to politicians from opposing parties discussing the latest government statistics on homelessness, inflation, unemployment, by-election results – take your choice.

This book aims to teach not only the methods, but to indicate the limitations of statistical methods and the proper interpretation of data. It will help you to evaluate other peoples statistics if you can understand how the data has been collected and processed. It will give you a healthy scepticism towards those who try to prove a point by throwing figures at you without any indication of how those figures have been calculated.

Statistics attempts to find out something about a population, something that cannot be known without enquiry, measuring and counting.

Statistical data collected as part of normal working may provide useful information, e.g. the daily recording of issues, reference library enquiries, numbers of readers joining, interlibrary loan requests, additions to stock. Information easily drawn from this could include:

- the average daily issue
- comparison of this year with last year
- ratios of fiction to non-fiction borrowed
- ratios of adult to junior stock.

As well as recorded figures, data may be collected from a survey. Choosing a week in the year which could be regarded as 'typical', every person (or tenth person, or 15th person) coming into the library could be asked 'How often do you visit the library in the course of a year?' The results may be dealt with at two levels.

1   *Descriptive statistics* describes what the data show. There is no estimation, no questions of confidence or probability. The survey may enable us to make statements such as '5% of the respondents used the library 15 times' or 'the mean number of visits was 25'.

These statements might be taken as indicators of overall library use, with some common-sense reservations (e.g. awareness of slack times and busy times).

2   *Inferential statistics* attempts to do more than say things about the sample. It tries to make statements about the parent population from the evidence of the sample. A typical statement would be 'I am 95% confident that the true mean number of visits is somewhere between 22 and 25 per week'. This kind of conclusion is based on probability – the answer is probably correct 95% of the time but there is a 5% probability that it is not correct.

When we look at any data that are collected by survey we need to be aware of some problems. When was the survey conducted and by whom? In our example if the survey was conducted on the week before Christmas we may expect the results to be lower than if it was conducted in the middle of the Easter vacation. Equally if the survey was asking for critical evaluation of the library service the fact that it was handed out and collected by 'that nice gentleman on the issue desk' may influence the freedom with which the respondents answered the question.

We recently heard of a library survey, part of which asked how the public rated the fax facilities. The librarian was particularly pleased with the high level of satisfaction (70%) especially as the library in question did not have a fax machine!

There may be many reasons for that error (the readers were confused by the question, they didn't want to offend the librarian, or they may have confused faxing with photocopying etc.). It serves, however, to illustrate how careful one has to be in designing and carrying out surveys.

Statistics correctly collected may be used to illuminate management decisions – correlating the figures with data about costs, staffing, opening hours, service points, demographic details and other factors.

One also needs to be aware of who is asking the question and why. It may shock some of you to realize this but not everyone is honest when presenting findings! Be aware of what they are omitting to tell you. For example, a study may show that workers in a particular industry appear to be less susceptible to a disease that has been associated with their occupation. This information should be treated with some caution if it was presented by the directors of the company that employed the workers.

One would need to know how the survey was carried out, the age of the workers, how long they had been employed in that occupation and, most importantly, how long it was before the symptoms of the disease manifested themselves. If the disease developed after ten years and the survey was of a group of workers who had only been in that occupation for four years one should query the validity of the results.

Always make sure that the statistician is comparing like with like. Has there been any change in the population since the last survey? Are unemployment figures in 1995 calculated on the same basis as they were in 1989?

Always be aware that in surveys people often give the answer they feel is appropriate. For instance, some doctors have said that most people underestimate their consumption of alcohol and tobacco but overestimate the amount of physical exercise they take.

Try to find out *why* the survey was conducted. If people are being surveyed for tax relief they are more likely to emphasize their expenditure and financial commitments than they would if they were being questioned over ability to repay a bank loan. It's only human nature!

Be wary of data that come with a spurious professional qualification. A friend, a professional guitarist, has a PhD in music. He purchased it from an overseas university and has the right to call himself Doctor of Astral Harmony. He only uses it for amusement but it has been known for unscrupulous people to invent degrees (and even universities). Beware.

Develop a healthy mistrust for data that you have not collected and analysed yourself.

Having made you aware of the pitfalls of statistics it is worth repeating that statistics properly collected and analysed can be of great help to the information professional.

Statistics fulfil four main functions:

1   They reduce a large amount of information into a manageable size for presentation.

2   They provide an estimate of unknown values based on data at hand. How far can sample results of the population be predicated?

3   They can determine to what extent a hypothesis or series of hypotheses can be supported.

4   They can provide an estimate of the risk involved in accepting hypotheses as a basis for taking decisions and actions.

Groups and individuals can abuse statistical processes in three main ways:

1   By they way they collect the data.
2   By the way they analyse the figures.
3   By the way they present the information.

1   The way the data is collected. How have they asked the question? Many questions beg the answer yes. For instance 'Is your consumption of alcohol the same as the national average?' It would take a brave individual to answer 'No. More than double'.

When did they ask the question? As has already been illustrated the timing of questions can influence results. One could choose to survey the response to the opening of a new night club in a particular area. If you chose to question pedestrians in the area at 1.45 a.m. you would be surveying a different population than if you asked the same question at 9.30 a.m.

Whom did they ask? If a survey was undertaken on the potential of bringing back the death penalty in Britain one may expect a different response from the police service from one taken from a population of 'lifers'.

Who asked the question? Do they have any particular axe to grind? Are they likely to have some sort of reward for the 'correct' response?

Most importantly why did they ask the question?

2   The way the figures are analysed. Have the correct and most appropriate methods been used? Has the process skewed the figures at all? These issues will be covered in more depth in later chapters.

3   The way the information is presented. Is the interpretation correct? For instance, you could have a population breakdown thus:

Income £20,000: 30%
Income £12,000: 25%
Income £8,000: 25%
Income <£5,000: 20%

interpreted as 'the highest percentage of the population had an income of £20,000' while the figures say that 70% of the population has an income of £12,000 or less.

Have they tried to distort the information by omitting areas of study? What percentage of the population did not respond? If you surveyed 100 people and had ten responses, all agreeing with the question, you could say '100% of all respondents agreed . . .'. What about the 90% that didn't respond?

Do the graphs accurately reflect the data? This is one of the easiest ways to distort the findings. Figure 1.1 shows how a sales executive would present his 'improvement in sales completed' to his manager. Note that the horizontal axis has no scale.

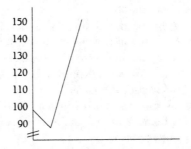

Fig. 1.1   Increase in sales completed, Agent Brown

Figure 2.2 shows the reality. Always look at any form of graphic representation very carefully.

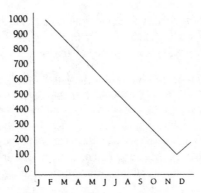

Fig. 1.2   Sales for Agent Brown 1994

7

Chapter 2
Elements of statistics

Summary

This chapter introduces you to the basic terminology in statistics and some mathematics.

At the conclusion of the chapter you should be able to understand the meaning of various statistical terms and symbols. You should be able to distinguish between the different types of variable (continuous, discrete, dependent and independent) and understand the various levels of measurement (nominal, ordinal, interval and ratio) and begin to see what can be done with them. You are reminded of some important basic arithmetic operations.

In this chapter we will be studying statistical terminology and levels of measurement.

Terminology

As with every specialist discipline statistics has it own terminology, therefore before we attempt to use statistics we have to understand its language.

To begin we will look at some key terms.

Population. This is the term used to denote all the units of analysis (elements) that might be investigated. Depending on your study a population could consist of people, libraries, books, shoes, hamsters, light-bulbs, television sets, water filters. All the objects about which we gather information is the 'population'.

The population does not have to be the total population (all women, all men, all librarians) it can be made up of all or some of a defined group e.g. all women in senior management positions, all men from a particular geographic area, all librarians working in academic libraries.

The population is all the cases to which statisticians wants their estimates to apply.

An example could be the learning ability of all white mice (or university students), or how long a water filter will be effective.

To take the water filter as an example, as a manufacturer of water filters you would like to know how long the filter will purify water. All our own produced water filters are our population. We set up our experiment. First we collect all our filters and start to use them and watch to see how long they continue to purify. Any problems?

If you are testing to destruction what do you have left to sell?

The solution to this problem is to select a sample. For example, it isn't necessary to drink a whole bottle of wine to ascertain if it is palatable, a sip (or glass) would suffice. So with statistical analysis. If the sample is correct we can make inferences for the whole population.

Sample. A sample is those units of analysis selected (in some appropriate way; see Chapter 10) for investigation. Appropriate samples save time and expense for the researcher.

For example, we could say that if the population consists of users of university libraries, the sample may be 2000 users selected in some appropriate way.

By studying these users we may find that one of our sample behaves differently to the majority and skews the data by taking out 'restricted access' books twice a year. So we look at this person in detail.

This person is known as a *case*. This case may be Fred Bloggs, Sue Hornby or water filter X4673, depending on our study. A case, therefore, is the generalized way of talking about a unit of study or observation.

What do we do with our sample once we have it? As far as statistics is concerned we reduce our findings to numbers that can be analysed.

Samples are made up of individuals: people, rats, light-bulbs, moths, potatoes, water filters. All members of the sample will share some characteristic in which we are interested. That characteristic could be colour, weight, sex, durability. Each case in our study will vary from one or more of the other cases of study in terms of this characteristic. For example some may be male, some female, some heavy, some light etc.

In looking at the members of the sample we are asking how they vary amongst themselves in one or more of these characteristics. These variable characteristics are called *variables*.

Variable is a characteristic or property of a unit (sex, age, number of books on loan) that may vary amongst the sample and population. It always amuses people when statisticians talk about populations broken down by age and sex, even knowing that this is a way of speaking about variables. There is still an abiding image of a Dorian Gray character!

Variables can be discrete or continuous.

A *discrete variable* is one in which the possible values are separated from one another, for example, in family size. A family may consist of one child, two children, but not 2.75 children. Another example may be the number of social workers in a town or the number of borrowers in a branch library.

A *continuous variable* is one where the value is continuous, for example, the length of hair, height of a tower block, weight of white mice. You can always measure an interval between the values of the variables.

Value. The score or value on a variable. **Take care not to confuse the value with the frequency.** For example, taking sex as the variable the *value* on that variable would be male or female, the *frequency* would be the number of each sex in our study.

Each variable for a case might have some specific dependent variable.

If we look at 'success in education' as a variable then it could depend on enjoyment of reading:

Enjoyment of reading	*Success in education*
Independent.	Dependent.
Variable	Variable

Independent variables can become dependent variables if the subject under study alters. Enjoyment of reading could depend on parental story-telling, which in turn could depend on tiredness of parent which could depend on hours worked outside the home, which depends on level of pay, and so on. Independent variables can become dependent as the area of study alters.

Frequency. The number of cases that share a particular value. If we take our value to be 'female borrowers' and in our study we have 120 female borrowers, then 120 is the frequency.

Looking at statistical studies, just as we have characteristics within the group that vary we will have characteristics that stay the same. These are known as *constants.*

Constant. A constant is a characteristic within the study that does not vary. For example, studying library borrowers we may find that they vary in age, sex, height, weight, ethnic origin but they will all share the characteristic that they belong to the library, that they are *Homo sapiens* and that they are alive.

The age at which people are allowed to vote is a constant, as is the maximum score available in a statistics examination.

So variables vary and constants remain the same.

We'll now examine terms relating to the measurement of variables.

Levels of measurement
Nominal (categorical)

This level of measurement is used when the values on the variable are labels only, when there is no inherent way of ordering, e.g. male, female, SF, romance, thriller, language, ethnic background. This is a limited way of treating statistics. Nominal variables are name-only variables.

Ordinal

This level of measurement is used when there is an inherent logical order to the value, an unequal interval, e.g. preference: 'I listen to *The Archers* never/rarely/ sometimes/often/very often.'

For example, if we had a sample of ten television sets and we have to rank their condition 1–10, the first being the best and tenth being the worst, what kind of variable is that?

It is an ordinal level of measurement. We can not say how much worse than the 10th is the 1st. It may be slightly worse, it may not be working. Ordinal is a logical ranking level of measurement.

Interval

This level of measurement has equal intervals on the scale but is set at an arbitrary zero, e.g. the point at which water freezes. The distance between each degree is equal but there is no true zero therefore we can have minus degrees. Another example is calendar years with Year 1 seen as the year of Christ's birth; before that is BC.

Ratio

This is the highest level of measurement. It has a logical order, equal intervals and a true zero, e.g. Degrees Kelvin has a true zero, as have length, weight, time and speed.

Interval and ratio are, for the purposes of this section of the text, treated as equal for use.

Questions

1 Which is a variable (V) and which a constant (C)?

Age of students entering University?
The age at which you become eligible to vote?
Score obtained on a 100-item test?
Maximum scores obtainable on a 100-item test?
Number of workers going to work on public transport?
Number of shares traded on the stock exchange on 3 February?

2 Is intelligence an independent or a dependent variable? (Intelligence is defined as scores on a standard intelligence test.)

Study A investigates the effect of intelligence on the speed of completion of a problem-solving test.
Study B investigates the effect of early environmental stimulation on the intelligence of children.
In Study A the intelligence is the independent/dependent variable?
In Study B the intelligence is the independent/dependent variable?

3 In the following story certain phrases are numbered and italicized. Each such phrase corresponds to one of the terms in the list below. Match the phrases to the terms.

A head nurse suspected that the [1]*200 nurses in her hospital* needed updating on antiseptic procedures. She did not want to test the knowledge of the whole 200 to assess the currency of their knowledge, so all the names were written on a piece of paper and put into a bedpan. A blindfolded porter drew out 30 names. These [2]*30 nurses* were asked to answer questions to see how much they [3]*knew about antiseptic procedures.* [4]*Nurse Pat Hughes* was the only [5]*one* to get all [6]*50 answers* right. The head nurse believed that this was because Pat had done her [7]*initial training* at the same nursing school as herself.

    variable
    dependent variable
    independent variable
    population
    case
    sample
    value of a dependent variable
    frequency

4 Which of the following variables would be measured on a nominal (categorical) scale?

    sex   temperature
    height   colour
    occupation   weight
    speed of travel   religious persuasion

5 Identify the level of measurement (nominal (N), ordinal (O), or interval/ratio (I/R)) appropriate to the following variables:

The concentration of fluoride in a sample of milk, in milligrams per litre.
The species of each insect found in a sample plot of farmland.
The reaction time of a subject, in milliseconds, after exposure to a stimulus.
Response to a question graded as strongly agree/agree/undecided/disagree/ strongly disagree.
The position of Liverpool Football Club in the League table, i.e. 1st, 2nd, 3rd, etc.
Body weights of hamsters.
Families by socio-economic status (social class).
Relative hardness of lead, iron, diamond.

6 Which of the following variables are discrete (D) and which are continuous (C)?

length of hair
incidents of disruptive behaviour
a library's acquisitions
amount of anxiety a person shows
intelligence
reading ability
library space per reader
number of doctors in a town

We have studied some statistical terms and levels of measurement. We are now ready to look at some data and try to make sense of it.

Maths refresher

This exercise is intended to remind you of some basic ideas that need to be second nature to you, and also to familiarize yourself with your calculator.

Calculators don't all behave in the same way, e.g. in the way they handle signs. Most follow the BODMAS logic (i.e. expressions are worked out in the order of brackets, 'of', division and multiplication, addition and subtraction). A calculator which does not follow this sequence will return some wrong answers unless you are aware of its own logic.

Example: $11 - 4 \times 3$ could yield the answer as 21 or as –1, after simply keying in values in sequence.

Simple calculators will probably obediently deal with signs as they are entered, i.e.

$$\boxed{1}\ \boxed{1}\ \boxed{-}\ \boxed{4}\ \boxed{\times}\ \boxed{3}\ \boxed{=}\ \boxed{\qquad 21 \qquad}$$

Scientific calculators will give precedence to the multiply sign, taking 4×3 as a unit and subtracting the result from 11, i.e. $11 - (4 \times 3) = -1$.

What matters is your *intention*. Do you intend to take 4 from 11 and multiply the answer by 3? If your calculator has brackets, use them, i.e. $(11 - 4) \times 3 =$, or take the entry of figures in stages using intermediate equals signs, i.e. $11 - 4 = , \times 3 =$.

More complex expressions, as in formulae, require care in keying.

$\dfrac{19 + 38}{72 + 68}$ entered in sequence is $19 + 38 \div 72 + 68$.

It is intended that the upper and lower parts of the expression should be evaluated separately, and then divided. The answer should be:

$(19 + 38) \div (72 + 68) = 57 \div 140 = 0.407$

A *simple calculator* will handle the values and signs in order, if keyed uncritically in sequence, giving

13

$$19 + 38 = 57, \div 72 = 0.7916, + 68 = 68.7916.$$

A *scientific calculator* would also give the wrong answer if values and signs are simply keyed in sequence, reading the expression as:

$$(19 + (38 \div 72)) + 68 = 87.527778.$$

The correct answer will again depend on use of brackets or intermediate equals signs or both, e.g. with a scientific calculator

$$19 + 38 = , \div [72 + 68] = 0.407.$$

These matters may seem obvious, and labouring a point, but most people will naturally trust their calculators and may not be aware of differences in the way that they 'think'. They will enter figures and signs and be confident in the answer that the calculator has returned. It will repay you to spend some time entering simple sums, the sort that you can do in your head or verify quickly on paper, and determining how to get the correct answers from the calculator.

Scientific calculators on the whole are good to have. They include functions which you will probably never need, but there are others which are very useful: nested brackets, factorial key, +/– conversions, raising to a power, and some statistical functions.

The exercises below include many sums that you could easily do in your head. Do them, then do them again with the calculator. Use this exercise to familiarize yourself with your calculator's way of working, as well as to remind yourself of some basic maths.

Evaluate the following:

1    $8 \times 5 - 3$
2    $8 \times (5 - 3)$
3    $2 \times 15 \div 3$
4   -14×14
5   -14×-14
6    $7 - 9 + 3$
7    $11 - 6 \times 5$
8    $5(3)$
9    $5(3 + 2)$
10    $-2(3 - 1)$
11    $(4 - 1)(8 + 4)$
12    $-6(227 + 258) \div 3$
13    $-3 - 4$
14    $2 \div 0$
15   4^0
16    $(-2) - (-3)$
17    $(2^3)(2^2)$

Express the following as percentages.

18 $\dfrac{2}{3}$ $\qquad\qquad\qquad$ $\dfrac{273}{100}$

19 Express 9 as a percentage of 40

20 Express 6.3 + 8.15 as a percentage of 38.3

21 Find 5% of £9.50

22 Express 83% as a fraction.

23 What is 4.885 × 24 correct to four significant figures?

24 Express 81 ÷ 0.07 × 2.33 rounded to three decimal places.

25 If $a = 8$, $b = 6$, $x = 9$ and $y = 4$, find the value of

$$\frac{5a}{3} - \frac{b^3}{x} + \frac{7y^2}{a}$$

26 If $n = 4$, $r = 2$, $p = 0.25$, find the value of

$$\frac{n!}{r!(n-r)!} \times p^r \times (1-p)^{(n-r)}$$

(See pp.75–6 if you are not familiar with the meaning of !.)

Exponents

Some calculators handle very large or very small values by expressing them in 'scientific notation', as they could not otherwise be displayed: 1,000,000 × 999 is displayed as 9.99 08. The two digits 08 are an exponent, and show that the true figure is obtained by moving the decimal point eight places to the right. If an exponent has a minus sign in front of it, the decimal point has to be moved the stated number of places to the left. Numbers appearing in this form can be treated as normal, and may be added, multiplied, etc. with 'ordinary' numbers.

Part 2
Descriptive statistics

Chapter 3
Percentages, proportions and ratios

Summary

This chapter introduces some fundamental methods of statistical comparison.

At the conclusion of the chapter you should be able to calculate percentages, proportion and ratios and be aware of their uses. Using imaginary but typical library statistics, examples are given of the use of these methods of comparison.

Statistics is often used to make comparison between similar yet different sets of data. For example, to compare the staffing levels in two different libraries, or the differences in budgeting between different local authorities. The simplest methods of comparison are percentages (%) proportion and ratio. They are easy to calculate and can give an overview of the data.

Study Table 3.1.

Table 3.1

	City	Newtown
Staffing		
Professional	28	72
Non-professional	46	143
Manual	18	24
Total	92	239

This shows the staffing levels in two different libraries. City has a total of 92 staff while Newtown has a total of 239 staff.

Using the raw data from this table we can calculate the percentage of staff in the three different categories (professional, non-professional and manual).

Calculating the percentage

The first step in calculating the percentage is to calculate *the proportion*.

In the above table from a total of 92 staff, City have 28 professional staff; 28 divided by 92 will give you the proportion of professional staff.

Here we can see the proportions of all the staff in City:

Professional	0.304
Non-professional	0.5
Manual	0.196
Total	1 (The sum should always equal 1.)

Proportions can be converted to percentages by moving the point along two places or by multiplying by 100.

Table 3.2 is Table 3.1 converted to a percentage table.

Table 3.2

	City		Newtown	
Staffing		[%]		[%]
Professional	28	30.43	72	30.13
Non-professional	46	50	143	59.8
Manual	18	19.57	24	10.04
Total	92	100	239	99.97

Where rounding causes a slight shortfall in 100%, or a slight excess, the difference can be added to or subtracted from the largest category, to make a round 100%.

Let us take another example. If a student had completed a piece of work and it was marked out of 15 and the mark allocated was 10.5. What would be the proportion and the percentage? First of all we work out the proportion which is:

$10.5/15 = 0.7$

What is that as a percentage?

$10.5/15 \times 100 = 70$

A first. Well done!

The next piece of work is marked out of 35 and the mark is 24:

$24/35 = 0.6857142$
$24/35 \times 100 = 68.57142$

A high 2:1. Well done!

Imagine the student got 14 marks:

$14/35 = 0.4$
$14/35 \times 100 = 40$

40% a bare pass. Squeaked through!

What is £6 as a percentage of £45? $6/45 \times 100 = 13.3\%$
What is 7% of £5? $7/100 \times 5 = 35p$

As a lecturer, you get an astounding project to mark and want to give it 85% of 35 marks. How do you work it out?
$85/100 \times 35 = 29.75$

Now let's look at ratios.

Ratios

A ratio is a relationship between two quantities expressed in a number of units which enables comparison to be made between them.

For example, two motor cars may be travelling at different speeds, say 100 mph and 50 mph. The ratio of the speed would be 100:50 or 10:5 or 2:1.

Let's look at the ratio of professional staff to other non-professional in the two boroughs we are studying.

City
Professional   28:46
Non-professional   46
Ratio of professional:non-professional = 28:46

Newtown
Professional   72
Non-Professional   143
Ratio of professional:non-professional = 72:143

This doesn't immediately give us a comparison between the two boroughs so we make one value similar. We make the figure for professional staff equal 1. We do this by dividing by itself and then by dividing the figure for other non-professional by the figure for professional:

City	*Newtown*
(28/28) 28:46 (46/28)	(72/72) 72:143 (143/72)
1:1.64	1:1.986

This is much easier to read and comprehend and indicates a significant difference. Despite the higher level of staffing in City there is a higher ratio of other non-professional staff to professional staff than in Newtown.

Although percentage, proportion and ratio are all useful methods of comparison care must be taken in interpreting the statistics. The bare figures we have studied tell us nothing about the level and age profile of the population they serve, nothing about whether one borough is a suburb, nothing about the level of funding available and type of library service provided.

Having looked at these simple methods of comparison try to answer the following questions.

Questions

1   Examine the imaginary statistics provided and attempt the following questions.

1.1   Look at the population figures. How would you explain the difference between City and Newtown? Can you say how many people moved into/out of these boroughs each day?

1.2   What can you infer about the figures for total book stock (any category)?

1.3   What do the figures for expenditure on salaries mean? What might affect the salaries of Metropolis as compared with Suburbia?

1.4   What is the total staff salary for City, based on the resident population?

1.5   Calculate the proportion and the percentage of staff in each category for City and Newtown.

1.6   Calculate the ratios for staff per 1000 resident population for City and Newtown.

1.7   What might the ratios on 1.6 tell you about the level of service in these authorities?

1.8   Calculate the percentage of stock for each of the main categories for City and Newtown.

Local authority	Expenditure per 1000 population		Bookstock				
	Salaries £	Premises £	Ref 000	Fiction 000	Non-Fiction 000	Children's 000	
METROPOLIS							
City	6,964	1,805	59	152	190	96	
Newtown	8,094	1,184	77	204	447	174	
Lib A	6,550	904	94	186	244	89	
Lib B	9,006	1,514	142	258	389	184	
Central	384,483	129,856	299	89	207	24	
SUBURBIA							
LIB X	4,600	708	88	268	247	132	
LIB Y	4,209	964	42	185	123	87	
LIB Z	8,118	1,859	819	379	784	188	

Local authority	Population		Staff in Post			
	Resident	Daytime	Prof	Non-Prof	Manual	Total
METROPOLIS						
City	127,700	136,200	28	46	18	92
Newtown	285,700	258,390	72	143	24	239
Lib A	202,400	184,220	48	90	19	157
Lib B	297,300	223,620	43	104	24	171
Central	5,400	207,041	44	78	4	126
SUBURBIA						
LIB X	244,200	231,650	36	86	30	152
LIB Y	183,310	154,225	29	48	18	95
LIB Z	396,400	590,800	79	294	116	489

Chapter 4
Organizing data

Summary

In this chapter we begin to look at ways of organizing data. The rounding convention is explained. This chapter also introduces the methods of constructing simple bar and pie charts. You are introduced to the problems associated with graphic representation and ways of overcoming and recognizing them.

At the conclusion of the chapter you are able to see some logical ways of presenting data. You should be aware of the reasons for presenting data in tables and be able to construct a table using a rational and clear layout.

You should be able to enter the data into a table and construct consistent and equal classes.

Constructing tables

Tables are used to aid the understanding of data and so should be as simple, clear and unambiguous as possible. There are a number of types and styles of table and it would be a good idea for you to look at tables from government publications (for example *Social Trends*) and CIPFA library statistics to become aware of the conventions of table construction.

Newspapers and magazines also publish tables to accompany articles as do independent researchers and commercial organizations. By studying these tables you will be able to identify both good and bad practice in table construction.

Tables are used to:

* present the original figures in a orderly manner
* to show a specific pattern in the original figures
* to summarize the figures
* to provide information which may help to solve a problem.

There are three things to consider in table construction:

1   Decide the type of measurement required for the kind of data used, i.e. whether it is to be nominal, ordinal, interval or ratio.
2   Decide what type of table it will be, i.e. frequency or percentage. It is not good practice to put them both in the same table as this can lead to confusion and misunderstanding.
3   The layout of the table.

Study Table 4.1.

Table 4.1   BA student data

Self-reported eye colour

	Frequency
Brown	26
Blue	14
Green	8
Multi-coloured	8
Other	10

$N = 66 = 100\%$
N = Number of cases.

Here you can observe seven necessary features for the correct layout of a table:

1   The table requires a number if it is one of a series. In this case 'Table 4.1'.
2   The table also needs a heading, in this case 'BA Student Data'.
3   The reader needs to know from where the data was obtained. *Self-reported eye colour*, as a response to a group interview.
4   The values need to be identified. Here the data are nominal, the values are the colours involved blue, brown, green, multi-coloured and other.
5   You also need an indication of the type of table. That is whether your table is percentage or frequency. Here we have a frequency table.
6   You need to let your reader know how many cases are involved your research. This is shown by: $N =$
7   If necessary you need to indicate how many cases are missing cases from the table. This is not required here.

How to organize the data

Usually data are arranged from the largest frequency at the top to the lowest at the bottom. However the bottom figure in this case is higher that the two preceding figures. 'Other' here would mean a combination of several colours (grey, hazel) and so logically it would appear as the last in the table.

What about a higher level of measurement? How would you arrange ordinal data?

If your question was 'Do you like sprouts?' and you gave the respondent five choices (strongly like/like/don't mind/dislike/strongly dislike), you can see that from 'strongly dislike' to 'strongly like' there is a logical order. Your table should reflect this logical order.

Table 4.2   Sprouts data

Do you like sprouts? (Questionnaire survey)	
	%
Strongly like	5%
Like	10
Don't mind	10
Dislike	40
Strongly dislike	35
$N = 180$	
No missing cases	

As this is a percentage table here you can observe another convention. The percentage symbol (%) is shown at the top of the column and against the first figure. It doesn't appear against any other of the figures in the table. This aids clarity of presentation as many % signs could clutter the table and confuse the reader.

How then you to get the data into a table?

1   *Count.* You decide the value (value classes) and use a five-bar gate system for manual counting. For each case within a particular class you draw a line, for the fifth case you strike through the four lines. When you start counting, each of these five-bar gates counts for five cases.

⊞⊞

2   Having counted the data you enter it into the table.

When converting frequencies into percentages you may find that this may result in a figure such as 7.11111139%. You need to avoid this type of spurious accuracy that can confuse the reader and doesn't make for ease of use. If you find that you have a figure like this you need to 'round' the figure either up or down.

Rounding convention

The usual convention in rounding figures is that 5 and over are rounded up and 4 and under are rounded down. There are 10 divisions in a figure and 5 is not the middle figure.

e.g. 0,1,2,3,4 | 5,6,7,8,9

We are usually considering rounding after a decimal point. Even with integers (whole numbers) the same rule applies. So we might round to 80 if the figure is 84 or less and 90 if the figure is 85 or more. By rounding up and down the figures will approximately even out. You must be very wary of rounding too soon as this will distort your figures in later calculations.

How to organize a larger set of data

If we take the question 'What is your age to the nearest year?' and we get the following 48 replies

11	20	16	14	23	31
15	5	10	13	11	17
26	16	14	33	17	24
17	18	21	18	15	16
22	14	15	14	10	27
10	13	12	10	7	20
16	18	21	13	19	25
6	11	15	17	12	15

we can see that the youngest person is 5 and the oldest is 33. If we subtract 5 from 33 we are left with 28 different data categories.

We now need to group the data into classes. That is, we take several values and group them together. Taking that data we can construct Table 4.3:

Table 4.3

What is your age to the nearest year?	
Age	Frequency
5–9	3
10–14	16
15–19	17
20–24	7
25–29	3
30–34	2
$N = 48$	

When putting data into classes, always remember the following points:

1 Seldom use fewer than six or more than 15 classes.
2 Make sure each observation will fall into one, and only one, class. This is a

common error when people begin to study quantitative methods. The classes above may have been written incorrectly as 5–10, 10–15, 15–20. In that case where would you put the data for those who defined themselves as 10 or 15?

3   Try to make the classes cover an equal range of values. In this case each class covers the 5 values (5,6,7,8,9 – 10,11,12,13,14 – 15,16,17,18,19, etc.).

If you change the same data into percentages you will end up with the following table.

Table 4.4

What is your age to the nearest year?

Age	%
5–9	6
10–14	33
15–19	35
20–24	15
25–29	6
30–34	4
$N = 48$	

If you add the percentage column you will find that it totals 99%; this is due to the rounding convention and is known as a rounding error.

Always try to make your classes logical. In this case we could structure the table in 5s or 10s giving five- or ten-year intervals.

Having placed our data in tables we can now look at another way of presenting the data; graphic representation. In this chapter we look at simple bar charts and pie charts and in the next chapter we will look at histograms and polygons.

Visual (graphic) displays

Displaying the data in visual or pictorial form involves using bar charts (graphs) and pie charts.

Bar charts

There are three types of bar charts: simple, compound and component.

The simple bar chart (see Figures 4.1 and 4.2)

The horizontal axis of the chart shows the kind of data you are representing. The vertical axis is scaled for the scores to be represented, whether it will be frequency or percentage.

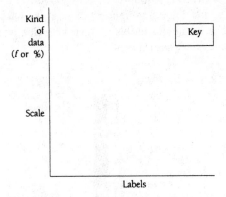

Fig. 4.1   Elements required for a simple bar chart

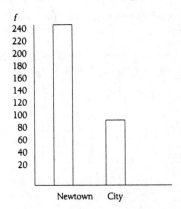

Fig. 4.2   Staffing establishments, Newtown and City Libraries – simple bar chart

The height of the bar represents the frequency.

As with tables any form of graphic representation requires a title and number if the graph is one of a sequence. In addition you need a key to indicate what each bar represents.

The main problem of bar charts is that the frequency is represented by the area of the bar. When comparing two sets of data you must ensure that you keep to a standard width of column.

Compound, or multiple, bar charts (see Figure 4.3)

These can provide comparative data, i.e. looking at data from two authorities on the one chart, by placing all component bars on the base line. You must use the same colour scheme and indicate this on your key. Compound bar charts can be used for both frequency and percentage tables.

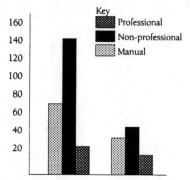

Fig. 4.3   Staffing establishments, Newtown and City Libraries – compound bar chart

Occasionally the lowest frequency will not be close to the zero point on your chart; in this case the convention is to use a broken line to indicate that the scale does not go from zero all the way up, e.g.

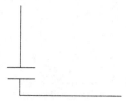

Component bar charts

These take each piece of data and place it on top of the other so instead of three bars you would have one bar divided into three parts. Again can be either a percentage or frequency chart.

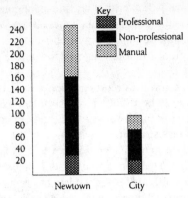

Fig. 4.4   Staffing establishments, Newtown and City Libraries – component bar chart

Pie charts

This is a circle divided into sections like a pie. It shows figures in proportion to the whole and in proportion to other figures.

To construct a pie chart it is necessary to calculate angles in the centre of the circle in proportion to the data concerned. As a circle has 360° we need to calculate the proportions as a percentage of 360.

For instance using the Newtown data we can see that professional staff make up 30% of the total staffing so the first section of our chart would be 30/100 × 360 = 108°. The full figures (rounded, since complete accuracy is unrealistic) are:

Professional	30%	108°
Non-professional.	60%	216°
Manual	10%	36°

See Figure 4.5.

Fig. 4.5   Staffing establishment, Newtown Library – pie chart

There are many problems of graphic representation. The drawing must not mislead or confuse. It is there to make the figures clearer. Make sure that the figures and the drawing are accurate and that both the horizontal and vertical axes are labelled clearly.

As mentioned before it is easy to confuse the reader by unclear and misleading graphs.

If graphic forms of representation are used imprecisely then problems can ensue. Details have to be exact and construction has to be as accurate as possible or the information may be distorted. This can be conscious distortion or inaccurate or badly constructed illustrations.

Squares on graph paper may cover a group of values. The thickness of the line can cover more than one value. In addition printed graphs often don't have lines. The graph, however, must be constructed as accurately as possible.

All forms of misrepresentation and ambiguity must be avoided as they undermine the basic intention of statistics which is to inform accurately.

Questions

1 The following are the results of a survey conducted to ascertain the age range of people visiting an exhibition of rare books. Everyone was asked to state their age to the nearest year.

27	27	42	37	27	37	62	17	27	32
42	42	47	52	17	47	52	37	32	57
62	32	47	37	52	37	57	37	22	42
32	32	17	52	22	47	57	27	27	42
52	42	32	42	27	42	47	37	47	52

Using these figures construct a frequency or percentage table.

2 Refer to the table of library statistics in Chapter 3. Take the stock holdings figures for Suburbia Library X and construct a frequency or percentage simple bar chart, a compound bar chart and a component bar chart.

Chapter 5
Measures of central tendency

Summary

This chapter familiarizes you with the use of the arithmetic mean, the median and the mode for raw and grouped data. We look at the advantages and limitations of each of the measures, their uses and values. We study frequency distributions and cumulative frequency. We review class intervals and class boundaries and calculate midpoints. We look at graphing interval/ratio variables using histograms and polygons. We discuss the accuracy and reliability of the various techniques introduced.

At the end of the chapter you should be able to calculate the three measures of central tendency, understand their advantages and limitations and present data as a polygon or histogram.

Having looked at organizing the raw data we can now start to make sense of them. We still have a lot of figures albeit in some order. We can now calculate what are known as summary statistics. These are single figures that summarize a lot of information into a single statistic. There are two types of summary statistics:

1 *Measures of central tendency.* These show the grouping together of the figures around some central point of the data. They are often referred to colloquially as 'averages'.

2 *Measures of dispersion.* This measures variability of the data; i.e. how great is the range of the figures.

For the purposes of this text the summary statistics that we will be studying in detail are:

Central tendency	Dispersion
Mode	Range
Median	Interquartile range
Arithmetic mean	Standard deviation

The arithmetic mean and the standard deviation are the most important of the summary statistics to calculate because of their value in inferential statistics.

Let us consider the three measures of central tendency in some detail.

The mode

This is the value with the largest frequency. In grouped data it is referred to as the modal class, that is the class with the largest number of cases in it. This class is presumed to contain the mode of the raw data. It is often used by non-statisticians in conversation. For example the statement could be made that: 'The average family surveyed had two children'. The arithmetic mean may indicate that the 'average' family in the survey had 2.3 children but logically that is hardly sensible. What is 0.3 of a child?

The mode then is the most frequently occurring value in a distribution.

Age	Frequency	Cumulative frequency f	
		< 5	0
5–9	3	<10	3
10–14	16	<15	19
15–19	17	<20	36
20–24	7	<25	43
25–29	3	<30	46
30–34	2	<35	48

Here the modal class is the age range 15–19. The mode can apply to all type of data: nominal, ordinal, interval and ratio.

What is the mode in the following figures?

4, 5, 4, 6, 7, 6, 7, 9, 7, 7, 9, 9, 3, 3, 6, 2, 2, 1, 3

By arranging the figures in order we can see immediately that 7 is the figure that occurs most frequently:

1, 2, 2, 3, 3, 3, 4, 4, 5, 6, 6, 6, 7, 7, 7, 7, 9, 9, 9

The mode can best represent the usual or most common item in a distribution as it is the value that occurs most frequently. It has very practical uses. For example, in manufacturing clothing many items are made to modal sizes. The disadvantage of this is obvious to those of us who do not conform to a modal size.

Modal information can be supplied quickly and easily. It is also has the advantage of being an actual value that appears in the data.

However there are problems with using the mode as it may not be well defined. On occasions there may be two or more modes in a set of data.

What is the mode for the following set of data?

3, 4, 5, 4, 6, 7, 6, 1, 7, 9, 7, 7, 9, 9,
3, 9, 3, 6, 2, 2, 1, 3

Again by arranging the figures in order thus:

1, 1, 2, 2, 3, 3, 3, 3, 4, 4, 5, 6, 6, 6, 7,
7, 7, 7, 9, 9, 9, 9,

we can see that 3, 7, and 9 each occur four times.

In addition, as the mode does not include all the values of a distribution (just the most commonly occurring) it is not useful if the distribution is widespread, as the extreme figures in the distribution are ignored.

As the mode can be an imprecise measure of central tendency it is of minimum use in further calculations.

Median

This is the point, the value, that divides the data into two equal parts. It is used for ordered sets of data. To find the median we firstly have to arrange the data in order of size and locate the value that cuts the data in two equal parts.

The median is the value of the middle item of a distribution when that distribution is ranked in order of magnitude. It is unaffected by extreme scores.

For example, the following is a list of books on loan to academic staff within the management team of a library school.

5 7 10 8 6 11 13

To find the median the data is arranged in order of size thus:

5 6 7 8 10 11 13

The median is the point that divides the data equally.

5 6 7 8 10 11 13

Median

The median can be represented in mathematical terms, i.e. as a formula:

$$\frac{N+1}{2}$$

In the above example where there are seven cases, the formula would be:

$$\frac{7 + 1}{2} = \frac{8}{2} = 4\text{th item}$$

Can you see any problems with this formula?

What would happen if the data set has an even number of cases, say six?

4, 5, 7, 10, 12, 14

Median

In this example the median point is a point where there is no data present, using the formula:

$$\frac{6 + 1}{2} = \frac{7}{2} = 3.5\text{th item}$$

We find that the median is the 3.5th item. This is represented by taking the two values on either side of the median and adding them together and then dividing by two to give the median point.

$$\frac{7 + 10}{2} = \frac{17}{2} = 8.5, \text{ the median value}$$

The main advantages of using the median is that it is not distorted by extreme high or low values. It is straightforward to calculate and it can be an actual value that occurs in the data.

However, it gives the value of only one item (the central item in the distribution). The other values, although important in determining the position of the median, do not influence its value. Therefore if the values are widely spread the median may not be characteristic of the data.

In a continuous series, grouped in classes, the median value is an estimate assuming the values to be evenly distributed throughout each class. However in reality the data may be grouped at either extreme of any or all of the classes. Taking the figures we used to calculate the modal class:

Age	Frequency	Cumulative frequency	
		< 5	0
5–9	3	<10	3
10–14	16	<15	19
15–19	17	<20	36
20–24	7	<25	43
25–29	3	<30	46
30–34	2	<35	48

The position of the median case for continuous grouped data is calculated by

$$\frac{N}{2} \text{ or } \frac{48}{2} = 24$$

The 24th person's age is the median age. This is in the 15–19 age group. We can see this by looking at the cumulative frequency column. To find a closer calculation of the median age we have to assume that all the ages are evenly spread throughout that class. The 24th person would be the 5th person in the group. We know this because the last person in the 10–14 group was the 19th and $24 - 19 = 5$. We also know that that person is aged more that 15 years.

The class interval of 5 years is assumed to be divided equally between the 17 people in the group and the 24th person is the 5th person in the group.

Therefore the median is calculated thus:

$$M = 15 + \frac{5}{17} \times 5$$

So the median age for this data is: $15 + 1.470588 = 16.470588$.

If we break down that calculation we can see M is the median, 15 is the beginning of the class, 5/17 is the class interval (5 years) divided equally between the 17 people in the group and the final 5 indicates the fifth person in the group.

The arithmetic mean

This is easily understood and calculated. It takes into account every item in the distribution equally. It can be misleading: if any of the items are untypically high or low the arithmetic mean will be pulled away from the central position to the extremes. The arithmetic mean can be unhelpful if it is a fraction when the variable is discrete, for example, the number of children per family or absenteeism of students in a statistics lecture!

The arithmetic mean answers the implied question 'What would be the figure per day/week/person/household if all the cases were of equal value?' It is the most useful of the averages and is fundamental to further calculations and inferential statistics.

The formula for the mean is:

<u>Sum of all the values</u>
  number of cases

Taking the following raw data of age to the nearest year what is the mean age?

11	20	16	14	23	31
15	5	10	13	11	17
26	16	14	33	17	24
17	18	21	18	15	16
22	14	15	14	10	27
10	13	12	10	7	20
16	18	21	13	19	25
6	11	15	17	12	15

$$= \frac{783}{48} = 16.3$$

37

Grouped data

Calculating the mean for grouped data can be more difficult.

We are used to turning natural language into symbols; most library/information workers would understand the following :

600.0359 Dewey
003.2714(42) UDC

Statistics uses its own symbols in formulae. The following symbols are necessary for further calculations:

$\bar{x}$ = the arithmetic mean

n = number of cases
Σ = the total of (the Greek letter sigma indicating 'sum of')

x = values

So the formula for the arithmetic mean is:

$$\bar{x} = \Sigma \frac{x}{n}$$

Class midpoints

How do we work out the mean for grouped data? When data are grouped, we lose sight of the individual values. For each class we have no idea where the data stand in the class; they could be at either end of the class or clustered in the middle. We therefore take an estimate of the value that equals the middle point of each class and assume that each member of the class has that value.

5, 6, 7, 8, 9, 10

midpoint
7.5

We calculate the midpoint by using the real upper limit and the real lower limit for the data.

$$\text{midpoint} = \frac{\text{Real lower limit + real upper limit}}{2}$$

$$\text{midpoint} = \frac{L + U}{2}$$

The symbol for the midpoint is x.

Finding the midpoint is a simple matter of subtraction and division, but it is also necessary to take into account the type of variable that is involved.

Data will be recorded on a continuous scale, i.e. a standard measurement such as the standard measurement 0....100 (or whatever number concludes your data). The data however will be either discrete or continuous.

Discrete data

If we record discrete data, e.g. 1, 2, 3, 4, 5, 6, etc. we have to remember that there are 'gaps' between the numbers, that 1 jumps to 2, 2 to 3, etc. and that they do not increase in infinite steps. The scale however has no gaps. Values of the variable must therefore be expanded to their real limits in order to close the gaps.

1 becomes 0.5 – 1.5
2 becomes 1.5 – 2.5
etc.

When data are grouped the groups have to be treated in the same way and expanded to their real limits.

Classes 10 –14, 15 –19, 20 – 24, 25 – 29, etc.,

have to be regarded as

9.5 – 14.5, 14.5 – 19.5, 19.5 – 24.5, 24.5 – 29.5. etc.

To find the midpoint the upper limit is subtracted from the lower limit and divided by 2, and this answer added to the lower limit:

e.g. $14.5 - 9.5 = \dfrac{5}{2} = 2.5 + 9.5 = 12$

So the midpoints will be 12, 17, 22, 27.

Continuous data

Where the data is continuous with no gaps, e.g. age, time, speed, distance, area, the class intervals are treated differently.

Class 10 – 14 means 10, 11, 12, 13, and 14 up to the point where the score becomes 15.

So the classes above become

10 – 14.9, 15 – 19.9, 20 – 24.9 etc.

In this case the upper limit of the first class is 15, not 14.5 and the lower limit is 10, not 9.5.

The midpoint of the class is therefore

$15 - 10 = \dfrac{5}{2} = 2.5 + 10 = 12.5$

There are times when scores on a continuous variable are recorded as discrete values for convenience, e.g. ages of dependents may be recorded to the nearest year so that anyone between the ages of 17.5 and 18.5 is recorded as 18.

To find the midpoint in this circumstance presents no problems: the data are simply regarded as discrete and the classes are measured from their real limits.

Now find the midpoints for the following table which was recorded as continuous data:

Age	frequency
5–9	3
10–14	16
15–19	17
20–24	7
25–29	3
30–34	2

Calculating the grouped mean

As the data are continuous you should have a table that looks like this :

Age	mdpt
5–9	7.5
10–14	12.5
15–19	17.5
20–24	22.5
25–29	27.5
30–34	32.5

The next stage is to multiply the midpoints by the frequency and you should have a table that looks like this:

Age	midpoint	frequency	Age (midpoint × frequency)
5–9	7.5	3	22.5
10–14	12.5	16	200
15–19	17.5	17	297.5
20–24	22.5	7	157.5
25–29	27.5	3	82.5
20–34	32.5	2	65
			825

Therefore to find the mean for the grouped data in the example given we divide 825 by 48 = 17.1875

To summarize: work out the mean for grouped data:

1 Work out the midpoints.
2 Make a working table.
3 Multiply the midpoints by the frequency.
4 Sum stage 3.
5 Divide the sum by the number of cases.

The formula for the grouped mean is:

$$\bar{x}_g = \Sigma \frac{f\dot{x}}{n}$$

Type of variable that can be used with each measure of central tendency:

	Mode	Median	Mean
Nominal	Yes	No	No
Ordinal	Yes	Yes	No
Interval/Ratio	Yes	Yes	Yes

Now that we have looked at ways of calculating the measures of central tendency, let us examine ways of presenting this data in graphic from.

We have already looked at the simplest form of graphic representation, the bar chart. We will now examine how to present histograms and polygons.

Histograms and polygons

A histogram is a form of bar chart with a scale that can be laid out in order for the classes to run along from each other. It comes from the Greek *histos* or mast – a mast diagram or bar diagram. It is more exact than the bar charts that we have already studied in that the width is proportional to the class interval and the area proportional to the frequency.

The simplest is the line chart, where the length of each line is proportional to the frequency.

A histogram is an extension of the line chart. It is similar to a bar chart but the blocks must be proportional to the frequency.

Figures 5.1 and 5.2 have been calculated using the following table:

Age	frequency
5–9	3
10–14	16
15–19	17
20–25	7
25–29	3
30–34	2

Points to remember when constructing a histogram (see Figure 5.1)

1   The horizontal axis is a continuous scale including all the units of the grouped class intervals.

2   For each class in the distribution a block or vertical rectangle is drawn extending from the lower class limit to the upper class limit.

3   The area of this block must be proportional to the frequency of the class.

4   If the class intervals are equal throughout a frequency table, then the height of each block is proportional to the frequency.

5   There are never gaps between the histogram blocks because the class limits are the true limits in the case of continuous data and the mathematical limits in the case of discrete data.

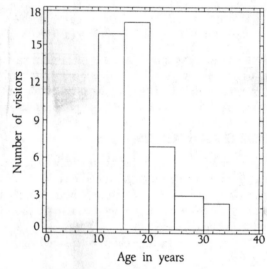

Fig. 5.1   Frequency histogram

Polygons

To make a polygon a line is superimposed on the histogram (see Figure 5.2).

To construct a polygon we must first calculate the midpoints of the classes as shown and plot the graph using the frequency of the classes. You will then have a series of lines joining the midpoints of a histogram. As with bar charts you need a consistent width, so with polygons.

The area of a histogram represents the area of distribution. Plotting a polygon at the midpoints will cut out part of the classes but will include other areas.

Histograms are plotted to represent the classes, polygons start and end at the midpoint of the highest and lowest classes.

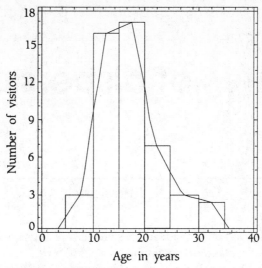

Fig. 5.2   Plotting the polygon

The beginning and ending midpoints of the graph are joined to the midpoints of the classes next to them, and as there is no data in those points it completes the graph. You are in effect imagining classes above and below the available data.

In theory a polygon is always drawn by constructing a histogram first; in practice, each point can be located by reference to the frequency and the midpoint.

Question

Using the following continuous data, calculate the mean, median and mode for both raw and grouped data. Group the data in classes.

    1–5
    6–10
    11–15
    16–20
    21–25
    26–30

16	23	21	11	18	20	17	19	18	14	23	18	13
22	22	8	22	20	22	21	17	10	20	19	14	12
19	11	21	23	13	18	26	12	10	5	16	24	14
22	20	13	25	21	19	25	20	15	11	14	20	17
5	13	24	16	16	20	18	19	13	23	16	7	15
21	14	18	22	15	29	13	23	15	19	20	12	16
24	22	20	12	22	7	5	28	19	20	13	14	19
13	12	17	28	20	21	20	16	21				

Chapter 6
Measures of dispersion

Summary

This chapter introduces the range, the interquartile range and the standard deviation.

At the conclusion of this chapter you should be able to calculate the three measures of dispersion and understand what they attempt to show. You should be able to construct an ogive and explain the use of the measures of dispersion.

In the last chapter we looked at how we can see how the data group around a central point and what this can tell us about the data. In this chapter we will find methods of calculating the spread of the data. The three methods we will use will be the range, the interquartile range (IQR) and the standard deviation.

The range

This is an everyday method of finding out the spread or dispersion of the data. It is easily calculated by subtracting the lowest value in a distribution from the highest.

For example, imagine that we have surveyed a fast-food chain and received information on the salary scales of a sample of employees from the chairman to the part-time sales assistant.

These are the random sample we are working with:

£3,000, £4,000, £7,000, £16,000, £20,000 £30,000, £38,000, £53,000, £61,000, £88,000.

The range is £88,000 – £3,000 = £85,000.

The arithmetic mean of this distribution would be £320000/10 = £32000. Therefore we can say that the company has an average salary of £32,000 with a range of £85,000.

The range used in conjunction with one of the measures of central tendency (arithmetic mean, median, mode) can provide a clear summary of the variation within any distribution.

The interquartile range

Any distribution can be divided into four equal parts, the points marking the division between these parts are known as quartiles. The interquartile range is the difference between the upper quartile (Q3) and the lower quartile (Q1). In effect what we are measuring is the spread of the middle 50% of the distribution. This has the advantage of excluding the upper and lower 25% of the distribution so any extreme values will not skew the data.

The interquartile range can be calculated by using two main methods.

Using an ogive

An ogive is a cumulative percentage or frequency graph. To draw an ogive you first have to produce a cumulative percentage or frequency table.

Produce a cumulative table

Age	frequency	%	cumulative %	
			<5	0
5–9	3	6	<10	6
10–14	16	33	<15	39
15–19	17	35	<20	74
20–25	7	15	<25	89
25–29	3	6	<30	95
30–34	2	4	<35	99

Taking the original data we add the percentage together. We can see that less than 5 years old is 0% of the data, less than 10 is 6% etc.

Plotting points %

Less than 5   0
Less than 10   6
Less than 15   39
Less than 20   74 —————— scale points
Less than 25   89
Less than 30   95
Less than 35   99

The cumulative table always starts at 0% and each point is arrived at by adding in the previous value. The ogive is plotted at the upper limits of each class.

You then lay out a percentage axis from 0%–100% and plot the ogive.

The polygon is joined at the midpoints of the two end categories containing no data.

An ogive is a cumulative (frequency or percentage) curve, a curve that represents how the data cumulates. An ogive can be used to estimate a median/IQR (see Figure 6.1).

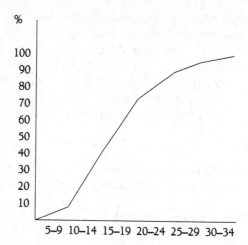

Fig. 6.1   Ogive

When you have your ogive plotted it can be used to estimate median, quartile (Q1, Q3,) points and IQR by dropping perpendiculars from the 25%, 50% and 75% points.

```
1/4  |  1/4  | 1/4  |  1/4
      |       |      |
     Q1              Q3
```

The interquartile range (IQR) covers the middle 50% of the range.

IQR = Q3 – Q1.

e.g. If the quartiles are Q3 = 27, Q1 = 11, IQR = 27 – 11 = 16

The interquartile range is not influenced by extreme items therefore very small and very large values do not alter its general spread.

The interquartile range can also be calculated without drawing an ogive.

For example, if we have a distribution of 20 people borrowing a different number of books during the year thus:

Borrower	Books	Borrower	Books
1	40	11	93
2	41	12	94
3	43	13	95
4	46	14	108
5	50	15	110
6	50	16	110
7	60	17	140
8	65	18	160
9	75	19	185
10	80	20	220

Borrower numbers 5, 10, 15 divided the distribution equally. The quartiles are calculated thus:

$$Q1 = \frac{n + 1}{4} = \frac{21}{4} = 5.25$$

$$Q3 = \frac{n + 1}{4} \times 3 = \frac{21}{4} = 15.75$$

So the IQR in this case = (5th person in the data and the 16th person in the data – with a rounding) $110 - 50 = 60$, so in this case the IQR is a range of 60 books.

The standard deviation (s)

The first thing to remember when calculating the standard deviation is not to panic! If you take it a step at a time and understand each part of the calculation (and more importantly understand what it is showing) it is easy.

Descriptive statistics can give an excellent overview of any distribution and the standard deviation is vital to that overview.

Neither the range nor the interquartile range use all the values in a distribution. The range uses only two (the highest and the lowest) and the interquartile range uses only the middle 50% of the distribution and this avoids distortion due to extreme values.

Like the arithmetic mean the standard deviation takes into account all the values in a distribution. It is important to understand the standard deviation because of its use in sampling theory.

The standard deviation can be used as a measure of dispersion in unimodal and symmetrical distributions; these are the distributions used in surveys and in quality control.

The standard deviation shows the dispersion of the values around the arithmetic mean, the greater the dispersion, the larger the standard deviation, e.g. a distribution with an arithmetic mean of 20 and a standard deviation of 5 has a wider spread than a similar distribution and a standard deviation of 3. This is shown graphically in Figure 6.2.

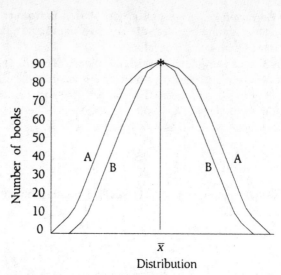

Fig. 6.2   Standard deviation distribution

Here we see that the distributions have the same number of items and share the same arithmetic mean but curve A has a wider spread than curve B.

This is a normal curve. With a normal curve it has been calculated that it is possible to mark off the areas under the curve into certain proportions.

Approximately 68% of the distribution will fall within one standard deviation, 95% within 1.96 standard deviations and 99% within 2.575 standard deviations.

Calculating the standard deviation

To calculate the standard deviation we take the deviation of each value from the arithmetic mean, then calculate an average from these deviations. Easy!

If you think about it, if the actual deviations from the arithmetic mean are all added together the result will always be zero as the positive and negative deviations will cancel each other out.

To illustrate:

For the values 6, 7, 9, 12, 16 the arithmetic mean is 10 (50/5).

Value	deviation	
6	−4	
7	−3	
9	−1	
12		+2
16		+6
	−8	+8

So the negative and positive signs cancel each other out. In order to find the dispersion around the mean the negative signs must be removed. As the song says we must 'eliminate the negative'.

In the standard deviation the deviation is squared. This has the effect of making the negatives positive. We then find the square root of the result to cancel out the squaring of the deviations. 'Logical', as Mr Spock would say.

It is logical and easy if you take your time.

The standard deviation is calculated by :

- finding the arithmetic mean
- finding the deviations from the mean
- squaring the deviations from the mean
- adding these individual values together
- divide this sum by the number of items in a distribution
- finding the square root of the result.

Let's work through an example.

Here is a list of books on loan to lecturers teaching statistics on 1.9.94

Lecturer	books	deviation		deviation squared
1	15	−5		25
2	25		+5	25
3	26		+6	36
4	20	0		0
5	14	−6		36
				122

122/5 = 22.4 and the square root of 22.4 is 4.9. So we have a standard deviation of 4.9.

Thinking back to our unimodal distribution one standard deviation should cover 68% of the distribution. In this example 15–25 books (20 plus and minus 5) is 60% of our distribution (3 out of 5) which is reasonable considering the small size of our sample.

It is important to note that when calculating a standard deviation for samples, a correction factor for sampling must be included. This is done by subtracting 1 from *n* so the formula will read:

$$s = \sqrt{\frac{\Sigma(x-\bar{x})^2}{n-1}}$$

Standard deviation for grouped distribution

As with the arithmetic mean the formula for grouped distribution is different from that for raw data.

The steps are as follows:

1   Follow the normal procedure to find the group mean:

  - multiply the class frequency by the class midpoint
  - total the values calculated in the previous step
  - divide this by the number of cases in the distribution.

Let's try this example. Calculate the mean and the standard deviation for the following data.

	f
5–9	2
10–14	3
15–19	5
20–24	9
25–29	7
30–34	5
35–39	3
40–44	1

We now have to find the midpoint, the midpoints multiplied by the frequency.

	f	$\dot{x}$	$f\dot{x}$
5–9	2	7	14
10–14	3	12	36
15–19	5	17	85
20–24	9	22	198
25–29	7	27	189
30–34	5	32	160
35–39	3	37	111
40–44	1	42	42

The sum of this is 835, which divided by the frequency (35) gives us a group mean
of 23.857.

2   We now need to find the standard deviation:

  - firstly find the deviation (each $x - \bar{x}$) and then square it
  - the square is then multiplied by the frequency
  - these final figures are totalled.

	f	x	fx	$x - \bar{x}$	$(x - \bar{x})^2$	$(x - \bar{x})^2 f$
5–9	2	7	14	−16.86	284.2596	568.5192
10–14	3	12	36	−11.86	140.6596	421.9788
15–19	5	17	85	− 6.86	47.0596	235.298
20–24	9	22	198	−1.86	3.4596	31.1364
25–29	7	27	189	3.14	9.8596	69.0172
30–34	5	32	160	8.14	66.2596	331.298
35–39	3	37	111	13.14	172.6596	517.9788
40–44	1	42	42	8.14	329.0596	329.0596
						2504.286

To find the standard deviation we then divide this figure by the frequency – in this case $35 - 1 = 34$. Find the square root of this and we have the standard deviation.

$$ s = \sqrt{\frac{2504.286}{34}} = \sqrt{73.655471} = 8.58 $$

Questions

1 Using the following table construct an ogive and use it to calculate the inter-quartile range:

Table 1.5

Age to the nearest year	
15–19	3
20–24	2
25–29	7
30–34	6
35–39	7
40–44	8
45–49	6
50–54	6
55–59	3
60–64	2
$N = 50$	

2 The times spent (in hours per week) in a college library by students were as follows:

11	4	2	8	8	6	11	15	10	9
5	11	7	12	6	9	1	9	16	10
9	7	8	4	11	10	5	8	18	13
17	13	13	14	12	12	14	17	7	10
3	15	11	10	9	8	16	12	9	9

Group the data into a frequency distribution using the following classes: 0–4, 5–9, 10–14, 15–19. From the grouped data, calculate the mean and the standard deviation.

Chapter 7

Time series, index numbers

Summary

This chapter introduces you to time series, trend analysis and index numbers.

At the end of this chapter you should be able to define seasonal, cyclical and random variation. You should be able to work out a moving average and a mean cyclical variation and cyclically adjusted figures. You should be aware of the limitations and advantages of forecasting using trend analysis.

You should be able to calculate base-weighted index numbers and describe how they will be useful for the library/information worker in planning.

Time series and trend analysis

Time series is a method of manipulating data gathered over a given time (weekly, monthly, quarterly, yearly, daily) e.g. library issues, employment, sales, inflation etc.

Trend analysis asks the questions how does the data vary over time? Is there a trend?

Very often the trend is obscured by some variation. Instead of:

the graph would appear thus:

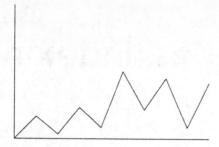

The data can be affected by many factors, e.g. unemployment rates can be affected by seasonal variations: more people work outside in the summer and there are seasonal jobs (in tourist areas), on the other hand many students are looking for jobs over the summer vacation.

Time series and trends are used for forecasting. Statistical forecasts are based on information about the way that variables have been behaving in the past and it is assumed that the patterns of the past will continue for a reasonable time into the future.

What is 'a reasonable' time? That depends on the variables; economic prosperity/depression/recession are usually similar over a period of years (despite the promises of politicians of any persuasion!), however umbrella sales may vary over days, weeks or even year (and in some summers even hours).

It is important to be aware that statistical projections do not necessarily produce accurate forecasts. To those cynics amongst you this may seem like stating the obvious but any analysis of trends depends on the assumption of political, economic, and social stability.

Trends can provide:

1   *Control.* This can be used for planning. They can indicate what has happened, how circumstances change over time. They are used in libraries for budgeting, stock holding and in business for market research. Governments use trends for forward planning controlling levels of employment, inflation, etc.

2   *Interpolation.* This is finding a value within the past trend which may be a guide for future action.

3   *Extrapolation.* This is extending a trend into the future to see what may happen. It cannot be emphasized enough that caution must be used in these circumstances. The variable may change, circumstances can (and usually do) alter and the trend may not be very accurate.

Most time series can be separated into clear trends:

- seasonal
- cyclical
- random.

Let us look at price as an example. The long-term trend is for prices to rise but there are cyclical fluctuations during which prices may fall or rise more slowly, e.g. seasonal variations, Christmas, summer sales, irregular variations such as shortages caused by strikes, poor harvest, increases in taxation.

Seasonal variation

As we have already said there are more jobs outside in summer (tourism, building). Within academic libraries issues fall during July–September (students are away for the summer) and the same effect can be seen in public libraries as people tend to read more in the winter.

Cyclical variation

This is variation over a period of years. The US business cycle is a good example of this. Just before the election for President there is a manufactured boom as the President attempts to inject money into the economy; that is followed by a clamp-down after the election.

Again, sunspots follow an 11-year cycle; this affects solar radiation which in turn can affect crops and the incidence of skin cancer.

Random variation

This is impossible to control. An example may be a particularly good summer that could affect the likelihood of people taking holidays abroad.

Time series attempts some techniques to remove the variation. We can manipulate seasonal and cyclical variations but not random variation.

The first thing we need to do is to develop a trend line, a way to handle the data.

Moving average

This applies to seasonal and cyclical variations and can produce seasonally-adjusted figures and trend lines. They are 'what-if models', e.g. 'What if it wasn't winter?'

In our data some figures will be above the average and some below. By using an average, fluctuations are offset one against another to produce the trend.

Normally the length of a moving average (two-year, five-year, three-year) will be based on the period of time between successive peaks and troughs.

We are going to work out moving average over a three-year period. The data for a series of years shows definite peaks and troughs, e.g. a three-year cycle in issues.

Year	Issues (000s)	
1981	250	Moderate
1982	247	Low
1983	261	High
1984	249	Moderate
1985	244	Low
1986	255	High
1987	246	Moderate
1988	242	Low
1989	252	High

If we plot these issues we will have a graph that looks like Figure 7.1:

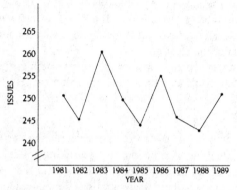

Fig. 7.1   Three-year cycle of issues in graph form

We need to calculate the average for each three-year period throughout the whole period. Starting at 1981, then 1982, etc.

We take the figures for the first three years and total them up. Thus:

Year	issues (000s)	3yr total	moving average
1981	250		
1982	247	758	252.7
1983	261	757	252.3
1984	249	754	251.3
1985	244	748	249.3
1986	255	745	248.3
1987	246	743	247.7
1988	242	740	246.7
1989	252		

The figures for 1981, 1982, 1983 equal 758. Divide that by 3 and we have a moving average of 252.7. The next set of figures are for 1982, 1983 and 1984, and so on.

Notice that you have no value for the first and last year in a three-year series.

If you over plot this on the graph the peaks and troughs will be ironed out producing a trend line as in Figure 7.2:

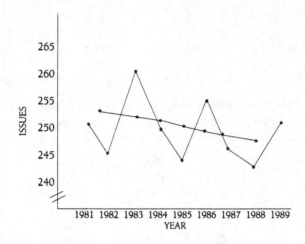

Fig. 7.2 Three-year cycle of issues – trend line

You can then extrapolate from the trend line to see what could be expected over the next years.

Using this technique we can produce cyclically-adjusted or seasonally-adjusted figures. This is an averaging technique that removes some of the fluctuation in the data.

Seasonally adjusted figures

We first need to calculate the cyclical variation (CV):

$$CV = \frac{\text{raw data (RD)}}{\text{moving average (MA)}} \times 100$$

In our example that would be:

$$\frac{247}{252.7} \times 100 = 97.7$$

Issues (000s)	CV (RD/MA × 100)	Mean cyclical variation (MCV)	Cyclically adjusted (RD/*Mean* CV × 100)
(1) 250		99.2	252.0
(2) 247	97.7	97.9	252.3
(3) 261	103.4	103	253.4
(1) 249	99.1	99.2	251
(2) 244	97.9	97.9	249.2
(3) 255	102.7	103	247.6
(1) 246	99.3	99.2	248
(2) 242	98.1	97.9	247.2
(3) 252		103	244.7

Here we have called the high year (1), the moderate year (2) and the low year (3). By adding the averages for those years together and dividing by the number of years you will get a mean cyclical variation (MCV) thus:

	Year (1)	Year (2)	Year (3)
		97.7	
	99.1	97.9	103.4
	99.3	98.1	102.7
	198.4	293.7	206.1
	198.4/2	293.7/3	206.1/2
MCV	99.2	97.9	103

This is then used to calculate the cyclically-adjusted figures as shown in the above table.

Let's now look at index numbers.

Index numbers (Price Index)

Index numbers are measures designed to show average changes in the price, quantity or value of a group of items over a period of time.

The aim of index numbers is to provide a way to simplify comparison over time. They replace complicated figures by simple ones calculated on a percentage basis (look at Chapter 3 on percentages, proportions and ratios if you want to refresh your memory). Most index numbers are weighted averages and thus have the same drawbacks that averages have. There are three types of indexes:

1 *Price indexes* which measure changes in prices over time.
2 *Quantity indexes* which measure production and output changes.
3 *Value indexes* which measure changes in the value of various commodities or activities.

The best known of all the indexes is the Retail Price Index a measurement of the cost of living and inflation.

As information workers we will also be aware of the BPI (Book Price Index), which shows how the price of books varies over time.

There are two types of index numbers, base-weighted and current-weighted. Both are usually aggregative.

Other textbooks may refer to the LASPEYRE index, base-weighted, price index.

We are going to look at base-weighted index numbers and the example used will be children's pocket money. Children usually like to spend their pocket money on sweet things, and our group of eight-year-olds are particularly interested in one type of chocolate bar, a fizzy drink and sherbet dips. We are going to compare the prices of these commodities over a period of time.

In 1980 SRAM bars cost 15p, in 1992 that had reached 30p.

	1980	1992
SRAM bars	15p	30p

To calculate the rise we divide 30 by 15 and multiply by 100.

$$\frac{30}{15} \times 100 = 200$$

This is the commonest way of calculation. (The US will sometimes use the base year as 1 rather than 100.) Here the base year number is 100:

$$\frac{15}{15} \times 100 = 100$$

Let's try another example using house prices:

Year	Average house prices (£)	Index number (price relative to 1980)
1980	18,000	$\frac{18,000}{18,000} \times 100 = 100$
1984	30,000	$\frac{30,000}{30,000} \times 100 = 166$

An index number above 100 indicates a rise in prices, below 100 indicates a fall in prices.

The formula to indicate the principle of calculating index number is :

$$I = \frac{P}{P} \times 100$$

or:

$$I_{84} = \frac{P_{84}}{P_{80}} \times 100$$

thus indicating the year using the subscript.

The base year can be indicated: 1980 = 100

More general symbols can be used :

$$I_N = \frac{P_N}{P_O} \times 100$$

O = year of origin

N = current (now) year, year of interest

Let's go back to the children's pocket money and calculate the value for different years.

	1980	1990	1992
SRAM bars	15p	27p	30p

Let's calculate the value for 1990.

$$I_N = \frac{P_N}{P_O} \times 100 = \frac{27}{15} \times 100 = 180$$

This indicates price relatives, i.e. the difference in the prices in two different years.

You can also calculate point rise and percentage rise.

The *point rise* indicates the difference in the index number between years.

The *percentage rise* indicates the percentage difference in the index number between years.

	1980	1990	1992
SRAM bars	15p	27p	30p
Index	100	180	120

Point rise between 1980 and 1990 = 180 – 100 = 80
Point rise between 1980 and 1992 = 200 – 100 =100

To calculate the percentage rise you divide the difference by the year and multiply by 100.

$$\frac{\text{Difference}}{\text{Year}} \times 100$$

$$1990 \quad \frac{80}{100} \times 100 = 80\%$$

1992 $\dfrac{100}{100} \times 100 = 100\%$

We can also compare 1990 to 1992

Point rise between 1990 and 1992 = $200 - 180 = 20$

Percentage rise between 1990 and 1992 = $\dfrac{200 - 180}{180} \times 100 = 11.1$

We can calculate more than one item in the index; we have already mentioned that children like to spend their pocket money on different commodities.

	1980	1990	1992
SRAM bars	15p	27p	30p
EKOC drink	40p	65p	74p
Sherbert Dips	1p	6p	8p

This can be calculated as:

(1992)

(Base year) $\dfrac{30+74+8}{15+40+1} \times 100 = \dfrac{112}{56} \times 100 = 200$

Formula:

$$I = \dfrac{\Sigma P_N}{\Sigma P_O} \times 100$$

This is the aggregative price index.

The child can eat more SRAM bars than drink bottles of EKOC (these are the large 'family'-sized bottles). So we need to look at the quantities (Q) consumed.

	$Q80$	1980	$Q90$	1990	$Q92$	1992
SRAM bars	(2)	15p	(2)	27p	(3)	30p
EKOC drink	(1)	40p	(15)	65p	(2)	74p
Sherbert Dips	(10)	1p	(15)	6p	(20)	8p

It is necessary to allow for difference in expenditure patterns when calculating index numbers. One consumes more bread than meat, one needs more tights than dresses.

Even though patterns of consumption change over time the quantities used are those of the base year so the index is base-year weighted, i.e. base-weighted.

$$\dfrac{(2 \times 30) + (1 \times 74) + (10 \times 8)}{(2 \times 15) + (1 \times 40) + (10 \times 1)} \times 100$$

$$= \dfrac{214}{80} \times 100 = 267.5$$

This assumes the same consumption pattern as in the base year. Why, do you think, is the current consumption pattern not noted? Because of the expense of conducting frequent surveys. For most indexes the base year is changed occasionally, e.g. every five or ten years.

Formula:

$$I_N = \frac{\Sigma P_N Q_O}{\Sigma P_O Q_O} \times 100$$

100 ————267.5 – one single value to express all the changes over a period of time.

Now try the following question:

The price of monographs in selected fields are noted and compared over a period of time. The average prices are shown in the table below.

Subject	Average price 1991	Average price 1994	Number of items in 1991
Science	£35	£45	253
Engineering	20	30	124
Statistics	12	17	54

From the figures calculate a base weighted price index where 1991 = 100.

Part 3
Probability

Chapter 8
Introducing inferential statistics and probability

Summary

This chapter introduces broad concepts of statistical inference, and those aspects of probability that are central to an understanding of inference. Studying probability helps to explain the behaviour of numbers and the assumptions that are made in inference and hypothesis testing

Inference

As stated in the Introduction, this aspect of statistics is about the measurement of uncertainty. What can safely be inferred about a characteristic of a population from the evidence of a single sample? Another sample might return a different result. Normally only one is taken, so how much can we rely on that one?

A sample is meant to be representative of the parent population from which it is drawn, so that what is true of the sample may be taken as true of the population. The chapter on sampling (Chapter 10) goes into details, but intuitively one can see that the sample should avoid an undue presence of one part of the population which would result in bias in the resulting statistics. For instance, library users of all ages should have an equal chance of being included in the sample. It does not mean that people of every age *will* be included, if members of the sample are randomly chosen, but that people of every age *could* have been chosen.

There are two related factors here: the variable being measured (ages of library users) and the units, which each possess a measure of the variable (the users themselves). In saying that all *users* have an equal chance of being included in the sample, it is also supposed that all *ages* have an equal chance of being included. We must be able to assume that the variable 'age' is distributed stochastically (randomly) around the population, so that in selecting a sample of 50 people at random, without prior knowledge of their ages or probable ages, every age score is given an equal chance of being represented. If these two assumptions are present – random distribution and complete randomness of choice of units of measurement – we can have a good measure of confidence in the representativeness of the sample.

Probabilities

We have to bear in mind probabilities. Our sample of 50 *could* theoretically have included 49 teenagers, instead of a spread of ages between the youngest and oldest. We would need to have some idea of how probable such a possibility would be. This can be illustrated with a contrived example (we have no official warrant for the figures) which will make the point. Assume that members of the Armed Forces range in age from 18 to 55 years, and assume that the great majority of them are between 20 and 35 years old. If this is true, a random sample would be expected to include more people from this age range than from above or below, simply because there are more of them. This is common sense. It is theoretically possible that the entire sample could comprise demob-happy 54-year-olds, but it is not so likely.

Population distributions

Any variable is distributed amongst its population with a mean value and a measure of dispersion (e.g. the standard deviation). Assumptions about the sample such as the foregoing one have some credibility if there is a definite shape to the distribution, e.g. a concentration around the mean value. The concentration could be towards one end of the range (army ages, the ages at which people take retirement from full-time employment) or near the middle (ages of library users). If the concentration is strong around a narrow range of central values, a sample mean will probably be a good estimate of the population mean.

Probability distribution models

The underlying characteristic of inferential statistics, however, is that we do not *know* the mean of the population or the dispersion of its values. If we had this information we would describe it and not be making inferences. We cannot therefore directly compare a sample with the population and see how alike they are. It is necessary to infer from sample to population through the medium of neutral, abstract model distributions of probabilities. Fortunately, mathematicians have supplied several such models, which will be met in later chapters. These models are easy to use, even if we can't understand the mathematics that created them.

These models measure probabilities of events. The section on Probability uses some down-to-earth examples to show that there are certain 'laws' of probability, and that numbers tend to obey these laws. 'Randomness' does not mean 'haphazard', and a properly-chosen random sample allows us to assume that the laws of probability are operating. As the mathematical models provide *measures* of probabilities, we can conclude at different levels of confidence that the sample *probably* reflects (or does not reflect) the population.

Two sides of inferential statistics

Inferential statistics seek to answer mainly two types of question, though in essence the two are very similar and use the same logic and tools.

How good is the sample as an estimator of the population?

If a reference library is staffed on a sample's evidence that the staff will deal with a comfortable average workload of 30 enquiries per day, how confident could we be that in fact they won't be inundated with enquiries on most days?

A pig breeder tries out a new formulation of pig feed and finds that his control sample brood are heavier than other pigs of the same age. If he marketed it nationwide, given the variables that obtain in pig-breeding, would breeders who bought it have the same results with their pigs?

Testing hypotheses

Here one begins with a belief that the mean of the variable in the population is already established. The mean number of pages in non-fiction books is believed to be a certain figure. A random sample of recent additions shows a larger mean number. Does this mean shelfspace is going to run out sooner than anticipated, or is there a difference in means only because random choice happened to have picked extra-thick volumes?

A borough's Works Department uses hundreds of light bulbs of a brand for which a design life of 220 hours is claimed. If a large number are observed throughout the town hall and libraries, and found to fail with an average life of less than 220 hours, should the director look elsewhere for light bulbs, or is the difference due only to the randomness of choice of the sample and the places where they were used, and therefore not significant?

These are the questions which occupy later chapters, but first it is necessary to digress into a consideration of probability. This is an interesting topic in itself and can (and does) occupy whole books. We shall be concerned only with gaining an instinctive understanding of the laws of probability and number behaviour that illuminate the inferential operations that will be described afterwards.

Some basics of probability

Inferential statistics depends largely on theories of probability. How probable (usual) is the result of a sample? How probable is it that we would get the same result, or approximately the same result, if we tried again?

Probability is the theoretical relative frequency of a certain event in the long run.

Theoretical probability

Theoretical probabilities can be worked out in advance and known exactly. The probabilities of picking the ace from a set of clubs from a pack of cards 1, 2, 3, 4 or 5 times is

1/13, 1/169, 1/2197, 1/28561, 1/371293.

There are a finite number of equally likely outcomes of an action, an experiment, a series of 'trials', a set of circumstances. We can know what *event* or *set of events* from amongst the sum of outcomes will give us a specific desired result. The desired result can therefore be expressed as a fraction:

$$\frac{s}{n} = \frac{\text{the 'success' or desired events}}{\text{the sum of possible outcomes}}$$

The simplest example is the tossing of a coin. The outcomes are only two, heads or tails. So the probability of getting a head is 1/2, or 0.5.

Rolling a die and hoping for a 6 has a probability of 1/6 and of getting an odd number is 3/6 but note that these probabilities only apply *in the long run*. Remember how long you have had to wait sometimes to begin a game of Snakes and Ladders! A throw of 5 will not necessarily be followed by a 6; a head will not necessarily be followed by a tail. The result is bound to be a head or tail *at every trial*, but as you know, a run of heads can be followed by a run of tails.

Some experiments you can do

Toss a coin 20 times and note how many heads you score. Calculate your score as $x/20$. You expect 0.5 as the probability in the long run: did it show in the short run? Do this again several times, cumulating your scores of heads, i.e. if in several groups of 20 tries each you scored 9, 12, 8, 13, 11, 10, 7. . . heads, calculate the cumulating proportions as

$$\frac{9}{20} \quad \frac{21}{40} \quad \frac{29}{60} \quad \frac{42}{80} \quad \frac{53}{100} \quad \frac{63}{120} \quad \frac{70}{140}$$

Your own figures might show a similar fluctuation, and it may be some time before you actually strike 0.5, but the fluctuations should mostly be close to the expected figure.

Practical probability

The theory is that all results are equally likely. Practical observation shows that sometimes some outcomes are more likely than others. The reason for this may be clear, or may not be. If you toss a coin twice, and you are interested in the joint outcome, you might find that you have

T   followed by T
H   followed by H
H   followed by T
T   followed by H

The last two are regarded as two separate outcomes, although both include one H and one T, therefore the H T combination is twice as likely to occur as T T or H H.

When sampling large populations, some outcomes are more likely than others, e.g. scores near the population mean of the variable are more likely than scores very different from the mean. As, however, a coin might give many heads before it gives a tail, in the short run, so a sample from a population might include many low scores before it picks up some average or near-average scores.

Another game you can play, is to roll two dice together. What you have to record is the sum of the two faces showing. Again, do this in several large groups, say 20 rolls each group.

This game is similar to the two-dice trials, in that not all results are equally likely. A score of 2 and 6 is not the same score as 6 and 2.

Possible scores range from 2 to 12. The ways in which these scores could be gained are shown in the Table 8.1. As you roll dice, tally your scores against each of the values 2 to 12. If you have no dice, you can still follow the argument. There are, as you can verify, 36 possible outcomes.

Table 8.1

					1,6					
				1,5	2,5	2,6				
			1,4	2,4	3,4	3,5	3,6			
		1,3	2,3	3,3	4,3	4,4	4,5	4,6		
	2,1	2,2	3,2	4,2	5,2	5,3	5,4	5,5	5,6	
1,1	1,2	3,1	4,1	5,1	6,1	6,2	6,3	6,4	6,5	6,6
2	3	4	5	6	7	8	9	10	11	12

The mean of this distribution is 7. Your expectation, in the long run, is that you would build up a distribution that is symmetrical like the model, having a mean of 7. You may be lucky and see the expected symmetrical shape emerging with your first set of 20 rolls. It may take several sets. This exercise was done with a group a few years ago. Three sets of results built up from a not-very-promising start to a close resemblance to a symmetrical histogram.

These games with coin and dice have a serious intent. Because we knew what we were looking for, we can see that the greater the number of trials that were made, the closer we came to the expected result. We can work out in advance the probability of rolling two dice and getting a score of, say, 5. Four ways out of 36 gives a probability of 4/36 which is 0.11.

The law of large numbers

As seen with the dice, increasing the number of trials resulted in a more accurate representation of the known distribution. In statistics, we will normally be in situations where we cannot know the total of possible outcomes. We take samples and measure a phenomenon in order to gain an estimate of that phenomenon in the parent population. A small sample (a few trials) may not give an accurate estimate. The accuracy of the estimate increases with the number of trials, i.e. with the size of the sample. An important embodiment of this fact is the **Law of large numbers**, which states that the larger a sample is, the nearer is its mean to the mean of the parent population.

Another form of *practical probability* which can be useful as a performance indicator is the form based on *observation*. In this, note is taken of the number of times a particular outcome has happened in a given number of trials, expressed as

number of times the result has occurred
number of trials

Interlibrary loans records may show that over the past year 70 out of every 100 applications met with success. The probability of success of any one application is therefore regarded as 0.7. Periodical checks can be taken to see if the proportion of successes remains constant, or has become higher or lower than 0.7.

Actuaries take note of such observed data in calculating insurance premiums. Here, the more information that is available the greater will be the accuracy of the estimate.

Mutually-exclusive events

If one event happens, the other or others cannot happen, *at the same trial*. A flipped coin will give a head, and cannot at the same trial give a tail.

p and q

In some statistical processes we have to take account of the probability that an event will *not* happen, as well as the probability that it *will*. A 'success' is complemented by its 'failure'. These concepts are notated by p and q.

Probability is expressed as a fraction of 1, because an event can only either happen (1) or not happen (0). Where an event will not happen at every trial (as with interlibrary loans), its probability is reckoned as between 0 and 1.

p is the probability of an event which would be regarded as a 'success'. If in a bag of marbles there are 12 green marbles and 1 red, the p of picking the red is 1/13 which is 0.077.

q is the probability that the desired event will not happen. It has the value of $1 - p$. If the red marble is the desired result, there are 12/13 ways of being disappointed and picking a green one instead, i.e. 0.923.

(Check that $1 - p = 1 - 0.077$, which is 0.923).

There is an analogy here with sampling. In a simple yes/no survey, if a yes is given, the same person can't give a no. Surveying is usually much more complicated than that, of course, since a question can allow a *range* of answers, but it is still true that if a respondent gives one answer (her age, the number of books read last month) she cannot give another.

Remember that p and q refer to the probability of an event at each trial. For each trial, $p + q = 1$.

Adding probabilities

We may be interested in the probability that a trial will produce *one of several* possible outcomes. The probability is the *sum* of the nominated outcomes, e.g. the probability of rolling a die and getting an even number. The three possible even numbers 2, 4 and 6 each have a probability of 1/6. In asking for 'an even number' we create a group of outcomes, whose

$$p = \frac{1}{6} + \frac{1}{6} + \frac{1}{6} = \frac{3}{6}$$

Non-mutually-exclusive events

There is sometimes an interest in having two or more events happen *together*. This called *joint probability*, and has applications in some statistical operations which will be met shortly.

If a die rolls a 3, could the next roll also be a 3? Possibly, because the outcome of one trial does not affect the outcome of the next. The outcomes are not mutually exclusive. At each roll, the probability of a 3, $p(3)$, is still 1/6. The probabilities of events that are desired together are *multiplied* to give the probability of the *joint event*. The probability of 3 followed by 3, $p(3,3)$ is $1/6 \times 1/6$, or 1/36. (Verify in Table 8.1 that there is only one combination of 3,3 in the 36 possible outcomes). This multiplication of joint probabilities explains the figures for picking the ace of clubs given earlier in this chapter.

The chances of a joint event are therefore *lower* than the chances of one of a choice of events.

The possible outcomes of a trial can be determined by a TREE DIAGRAM. Candidates for office in the Students Union could include four for President, two for Vice-President, and three for Treasurer. Each candidate for President, if successful, could be accompanied by any of the three Vice-President candidates, and so on.

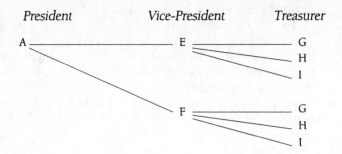

The full 'tree' would show the different combinations of 'names' which could constitute the winning three for these offices. To know how many combinations there are without drawing a diagram we multiply 4 × 2 × 3 = 24.

The probability of your choice, say B for President, E for Vice-President and J for Treasurer, is therefore 1/24. We could calculate the probability by recognizing that their chances are respectively 1/4, 1/2 and 1/3. Multiplying these to find the joint probability will give us 1/24 again.

It is important to be clear that joint probability deals with distinct events happening together. Suppose a university did a lucky dip of its 25,000 students to send some of them to Disneyland Paris. Three friends want to go together. What is the probability that all three of them would be lucky? Their chances are not

$$\frac{3}{25,000}, \text{ but } \frac{1}{25,000} \times \frac{1}{25,000} \times \frac{1}{25,000} = \text{a very slender chance!}$$

Independent and dependent events

If a certain event occurs, will it affect the probability that another event will occur?

A bag has 6 red marbles and 4 white. The probability of drawing a red is 6/10, and of drawing a white 4/10.

Draw a marble, note its colour, then replace it in the bag. Try again – the probabilities are still 6/10 and 4/10.

The probabilities attached to the second draw are not affected by the result of the first draw. The two events are *independent*.

This is an example of *sampling with replacement*. If, however, you take out a marble and *don't* replace it the probabilities on the second draw are changed. The probability of drawing a red on the second draw is 5/9 if the first draw took out a red, or 6/9 if the first draw took out a white.

These events are *dependent*. This is an example of *sampling without replacement*.

These thoughts should be borne in mind when reading the chapter on sampling.

The value of all this?

A wise man once said that the 'probable' is what usually happens. This recognizes that the probable event may not in fact happen every time. The exact probability of an event can be known, as in the case of coin tossing, but in the short run that probability may not be realized. We can't know in advance exactly how many Heads are going to show in a given number of trials. Probability is the *relative* frequency of an event in the long run (see the definition at the beginning of this section). How long is a long run? You might have achieved a heads count of 0.5 in a few dozen tosses. Others have tossed a coin 10,000 and 24,000 times, and found a relative frequency of 0.5005 and 0.5067.

The simple tests above show some important aspects of probability which are central to our purposes of inferential statistics.

1   The exact outcomes of a trial can't be known in advance, even if there is a theoretically expected probability.

2   A long-term order exists, which is seen only in the long run (in the pattern of results of rolling two dice), and revealed by many trials.

3   When the overall pattern is revealed, the relative probabilities of particular outcomes can be determined, e.g. the probabilities of rolling 2 dice and getting a 3 = 2/36 or 0.055; or a 7 = 6/36 or 0.166.

For the overall pattern to be present, the phenomenon must be truly random. Trials must be independent of each other, and the results of trials must not be affected in any way by interference. In sampling, this means that all members of a population must have the same opportunity to be included, and that every combination of N elements must have an equal opportunity of forming the sample.

The relationship of the foregoing principles to the sampling of populations is of great importance for inferential statistics. Researchers measure many phenomena in many variably-defined populations. A phenomenon may be distributed in the population in a regular, symmetrical pattern or with a skew. The distribution will not be known (or there would be no need for sampling) and even if it could be reasonably assumed, its precise properties and relative frequencies could not be known.

The answer to this conundrum lies in the way in which means of samples tend to behave. Assuming that all large samples of a given size from a population – or a very large number of them – were to have their means calculated, the means would be seen to tend to cluster round the mean of the population in a regular symmetrical pattern which would resemble or approximate to the Standard Normal Distribution (SND). The precise properties of the SND and the relative probabilities of stated outcomes are known. By using this distribution, statements can be made about the mean of a single sample, which would normally be all that a researcher takes.

(For application of the standard normal distribution, see the chapters on inference and hypothesis testing.)

Questions

1   The odds against Any Other Business winning the Derby are given as 2 to 1. The probability of winning is therefore judged to be 1/3. If the odds against Matters Arising are 5 to 3, what is the probability that the horse will lose?

2   Total probability, i.e. combining probabilities when *either* one *or* the other result would be regarded as a 'success'.
   If you were drawing one card from a pack, which of the following pairs of results would be mutually exclusive?

   a)   a diamond or a black card
   b)   a king or a red card
   c)   a 10 or a Jack
   d)   a spade or a black card?

3   Joint probability, i.e. combining probabilities when we want *both* one result *and* the other to occur in one trial.

   Library A has 14 staff, 3 of whom are men
   Library B has 16 staff, 3 of whom are men
   Library C has 15 staff, 2 of whom are men
   Library D has 16 staff, 4 of whom are men.

   Each staff acts separately and draws the name of one of its own members from hats. Calculate the probability that the libraries will choose an all-male group to attend the Library Resources Exhibition with expenses paid.

4   A machine that produces nails by the tens of thousands each day might produce 5% that are defective, as an average figure. Given that 5% are defective, what is the probability that an inspector, picking three at random from a batch of 1000, would find three defective nails?

Chapter 9
The binomial distribution

Summary

After studying this chapter you should have a better understanding of the ideas of probability introduced in the previous
chapter. You should also know more about probability distributions and the reasons why confidence can be placed in the
inferential tests which will appear in later chapters.

Here we meet and study the binomial distribution. In itself it
has limited practical use in library and information statistics. It
has great value in the learning of statistics. The concept is easy
to grasp and uses numbers that are manageable and compre-
hensible.

To approach the binomial distribution we need first to learn
something about permutations and combinations.

Permutations

Six horses in a race are simply six horses. If we are concerned with their order of
finishing, there are many possibilities. Ignoring possible influencing factors such as
training, jockey skills, 'nobbling', and assuming that all horses are equally matched:

- any of the six horses could occupy first place;
- for each of the six, there would be five remaining as contenders for second
  place;
- for each combination of 1st and 2nd places, there will be four candidates for
  3rd place; etc.

The number of possible finishing sequences (permutations of 6) is

$$6 \times 5 \times 4 \times 3 \times 2 \times 1 = 720$$

The permutations are expressed as '6 factorial', or 6!

It is often more useful to know the number of ways in which a subset of a group of objects could be arranged.

You have to interview six library assistants for three posts, one in each of three branch libraries. In how many ways, theoretically, could you a) select three people from the six, and b) distribute three people between the libraries? Each group of three has to be permuted 3! times.

The formula for *nPr* (the number of permutations of *r* objects taken from a set of *n* objects) is:

$$nPr = \frac{n!}{(n-r)!}$$

In the example:

$$_6P_3 = \frac{6!}{3!} = \frac{720}{6} = 120 \text{ ways}$$

This is not a practical way of approaching interviews, of course, but the calculation leads us to combinations.

Combinations

There are times when one wishes to know how in many ways *r* objects could be selected from amongst *n* objects, but the question of order is not important.

If you have to select three people out of four to give them a lift to a meeting, or to interviews, there are four ways in which three people could be chosen, i.e. four combinations.

If they can only be taken one at a time, and the order of arrival could be important, there are 24 possible arrangements, since each group of three could go in six ways, i.e. $3! \times 4 = 24$ *permutations*.

There are many more permutations than there are combinations of the same group of objects, since permutations of *nPr* give each combination *r factorial* times. The permutations formula must therefore be given an element which will divide permutations by *r* factorial.

Combinations of *n* objects taken *r* at a time is denoted as *nCr*, or $\binom{n}{r}$, and has the value of:

$$\binom{n}{r} = \frac{n!}{r! \times (n-r)}$$

A Schools Service Librarian has four copies of a book to be placed amongst 12 schools. In how many ways could these books be placed?

$$\binom{n}{r} = \binom{12}{4} + \frac{12!}{4! \times 8!} = \frac{12.11.10.9.8.7.6.5.4.3.2.1}{(4.3.2.1.) \times (8.7.6.5.4.3.2.1)}$$

As 8! (i.e. 8.7.6.5.4.3.2.1.) in the bottom line cancels out the same figures in the top line, the expression simplifies to

$$\frac{12.11.10.9}{4.3.2.1} = \frac{11880}{24} = 495 \text{ ways}$$

Another example involves the multiplication of probabilities met earlier.

An external examiner wants to see a randomly-selected sample of a class's research methods essays. He wants to see only six essays. There are 45 from which to choose. Of the 45, five have a fail mark. What is the probability that a random sample of six essays will *not* include a failed essay?

Method:

1 determine how many combinations of six are possible from 45;
2 determine how many combinations of six *passes* are possible (from 40);
3 express the desirable outcome as $\frac{s}{n}$.

All combinations of six, including failed scripts:

$$\binom{45}{6} = \frac{45!}{6! \times 39!} = \frac{45.44.43.42.41.40}{6.5.4.3.2.1} = \frac{5.86444\mathrm{E}09}{720} = 8145060$$

All combinations of six with no failed scripts:

$$\binom{40}{6} = \frac{40.39.38.37.36.35}{6.5.4.3.2.1} = \frac{2.76363\mathrm{E}09}{720} = 3838380$$

The probability therefore of no failed scripts is

$$\frac{s}{n} = \frac{3838380}{8145060} = 0.47$$

(The E in two of the figures above is an exponent. Refer to the maths revision in Chapter 2).

The binomial distribution

An event has a total probability of 1, as we've seen. If the probability of an event is less than 1, the total of 1 is made up of the 'success' and the 'failure'. Sometimes we want to make a number of trials and calculate the probability of success in none, 1, 2, 3, etc. of these trials. If, for instance, 12 orders are sent to an overseas bookseller, what are the chances of having 7 of the orders filled within six weeks?

The binomial ('two names') distribution deals with trials to which there can only be two outcomes:

- a coin will show heads or tails
- a birth will be a girl or a boy
- a question must be answered with Yes or No

- an order will be filled within six weeks or it will not.

Ground rules for the binomial distribution are

- each trial must have two mutually-exclusive outcomes
- one outcome will be regarded as a 'success'
- p(success) must be constant for each trial
- trials are independent: the outcome of each is not determined or influenced by what has happened before.

A candidate sits examinations in four subjects. At each sitting the result may be Pass or Fail. There are numerous possible sequences of P and F.

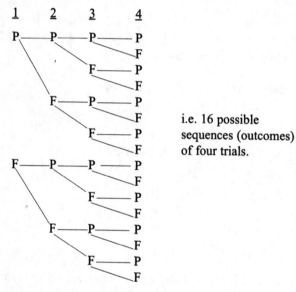

i.e. 16 possible
sequences (outcomes)
of four trials.

Although the two outcomes of 1 trial are equally likely, not all outcomes of *n* trials are equally likely.

Tracing along all the lines and branches above, we can count the incidences of outcomes as below:

P4	P3 F1	P2 F2	P1 F3	P0
1	4	6	4	1

The figures 1, 4, 6, 4, 1 are called the *binomial coefficients* of the outcomes of 4 trials, and show in how many ways the different *combinations* of P and F could occur. Statistical tables or textbooks may include a table of binomial coefficients. If not, they can be worked out with the combinations formula seen earlier, e.g. the number of ways of gaining two successes in four trials (i.e. P2 F2) is the same as looking at the combinations of four taken two at a time, or $\binom{4}{2}$.

Work this out and verify that the answer is 6. The formula for calculating binomial probabilities is:

$$p(r \text{ successes}) = \binom{n}{r} \times p^r \times q^{n-r}$$

In the Pass–Fail example, where $p = 0.5$ and q also $= 0.5$ the probability of gaining two passes in four trials would be calculated as

$$\binom{4}{2} \times (0.5)^2 \times (0.5)^2$$

$$= 6 \times (0.5)^2 \times (0.5)^2$$

$$= 0.375 = \frac{6}{16}$$

General application of the binomial distribution

The theory can be generalized to any number of trials, to any number of desired successes, and to any value of the probability of the desired event.

We must know the constant probability of a success at each trial (known from previous trials);

- the probability of a single event is p
- the probability that the event will *not* happen is q, (or $1 - p$).

The event is to happen r times, expressed as p'

The event will therefore not happen $n - r$ times, expressed as q^{n-r}.

The formula for the probability of r successes in n independent trials ($p(r)$) is built up from these elements, as seen above.

This formula makes use of joint probability, the probability that certain events will occur together, and involves multiplying together the probabilities of each event.

A college's records show that over many years students have come predominantly from the Northwest (75%) with 25% of students from elsewhere. What is the probability that five students chosen at random from a class of 12 will have come from the Northwest?

a) There are many ways of drawing 5 from 12, so $\binom{n}{r} = \binom{12}{5}$

b) The probability that *one* student has come from the Northwest is 0.75,
so $p(5) = 0.75 \times 0.75 \times 0.75 \times 0.75 \times 0.75 = p'$ or $(0.75)^5$

c) The probability that *one* student does *not* come from the Northwest is 0.25,
so $q(7) = 0.25 \times 0.25 \times 0.25 \times 0.25 \times 0.25 \times 0.25 \times 0.25$
$= q^{n-r}$ or $(0.25)^7$

The formula is

$$\binom{12}{5} \times (0.75)^5 \times (0.25)^7$$
$$= 792 \times 0.2373 \times 0.000061$$
$$= 0.0115$$

Distributions

While we speak of the binomial distribution, there is in fact a family of distributions, the properties of each distribution depending firstly on the probability of a single event, and secondly on the number of trials involved.

The notion that a variable is distributed among a population, that is, it can show a range of values, is an important one for us. A sample is a group of 'trials', and each sample would have its own mean. In usual terms, we would be interested to know how closely the mean of the sample approaches the mean of the population.

Example

Imagine that a librarian wants to form a temporary advisory group from the readership, to air and discuss some ideas for the development of the service. Eight people will be chosen by random selection from the readership records.

The readership is known to be approximately 1 ethnic minority member to 4 native white members, i.e. p (ethnic) = 1/5, and p (native) = 4/5. What are the possible combinations of native : ethnic, and how probable would each mix be? Results could range from 8 successes and 0 failures to 8 failures and 0 successes. Using 'success' and 'failure' with their purely statistical meanings, and nominating ethnic as a success and native as a failure, the distribution of possible outcomes, with their binomial coefficients and associated probabilities is as follows:

Table 9.1

Success Failure			p
8–0	$\binom{8}{8}$	$= 1 \times \frac{1}{5} \times \frac{1}{5} \times \frac{1}{5} \times \frac{1}{5} \times \frac{1}{5} \times \frac{1}{5} \times \frac{1}{5} \times \frac{1}{5}$	$= \frac{1}{390625}$
7–1	$\binom{8}{7}$	$= 8 \times \frac{4}{5} \times \frac{1}{5} \times \frac{1}{5} \times \frac{1}{5} \times \frac{1}{5} \times \frac{1}{5} \times \frac{1}{5} \times \frac{1}{5}$	$= \frac{32}{390625}$
6–2	$\binom{8}{6}$	$= 28 \times \frac{4}{5} \times \frac{4}{5} \times \frac{1}{5} \times \frac{1}{5} \times \frac{1}{5} \times \frac{1}{5} \times \frac{1}{5} \times \frac{1}{5}$	$= \frac{448}{390625}$
5–3	$\binom{8}{5}$	$= 56 \times \frac{4}{5} \times \frac{4}{5} \times \frac{4}{5} \times \frac{1}{5} \times \frac{1}{5} \times \frac{1}{5} \times \frac{1}{5} \times \frac{1}{5}$	$= \frac{3584}{390625}$
4–4	$\binom{8}{4}$	$= 70 \times \frac{4}{5} \times \frac{4}{5} \times \frac{4}{5} \times \frac{4}{5} \times \frac{1}{5} \times \frac{1}{5} \times \frac{1}{5} \times \frac{1}{5}$	$= \frac{17920}{390625}$
3–5	$\binom{8}{3}$	$= 56 \times \frac{4}{5} \times \frac{4}{5} \times \frac{4}{5} \times \frac{4}{5} \times \frac{4}{5} \times \frac{1}{5} \times \frac{1}{5} \times \frac{1}{5}$	$= \frac{57344}{390625}$
2–6	$\binom{8}{2}$	$= 28 \times \frac{4}{5} \times \frac{4}{5} \times \frac{4}{5} \times \frac{4}{5} \times \frac{4}{5} \times \frac{4}{5} \times \frac{1}{5} \times \frac{1}{5}$	$= \frac{114688}{390625}$
1–7	$\binom{8}{1}$	$= 8 \times \frac{4}{5} \times \frac{4}{5} \times \frac{4}{5} \times \frac{4}{5} \times \frac{4}{5} \times \frac{4}{5} \times \frac{4}{5} \times \frac{1}{5}$	$= \frac{131072}{390625}$
0–8	$\binom{8}{0}$	$= 1 \times \frac{4}{5} \times \frac{4}{5} \times \frac{4}{5} \times \frac{4}{5} \times \frac{4}{5} \times \frac{4}{5} \times \frac{4}{5} \times \frac{4}{5}$	$= \frac{65536}{390625}$

NB: 1 The coefficients are symmetrical:

   1 8 28 56 70 56 28 8 1

   2 Add the numerators on the right $= \frac{390625}{390625} = 1$

   3 Table 9.1 holds no surprises. As the probability of a success was only 0.2, the chances of 7 or 8 successes were therefore low. The distribution of probabilities of success peaks at the second and third lines from the bottom, i.e. about 1/5th the way up the column. The peak doesn't correspond exactly to any one line, but it is close enough to show that the distribution matches the expectation that $p = 0.2$ (1/5).

This table could have been worked out with the binomial distribution formula, given that $p(\text{success}) = 0.2$.

The value of the binomial distribution

It illustrates a lot of the important fundamental ideas of *probability* and *inference*. These ideas are vital for understanding the tests which we shall learn later.

1 Each trial must have *mutually-exclusive outcomes* (2 in the case of the binomial distribution).
2 $p(\text{success})$ is constant for each trial.
3 Trials are *independent*. The outcome of each one is by chance only.

We have seen some similarities with random sampling. Because we can see the effects of putting figures in and working with them we can see several ideas:-

4 The idea of a *distribution* of probabilities;
5 That the sum of all probabilities is 1;
6 The shape of the distribution depends on the value of $p(\text{success})$:

   • If $p = 0.2$ there is a skewed distribution
   • If $p = 0.5$ there is a symmetrical distribution.

7 A trial can produce one of a range of possible outcomes. This is similar to the idea that a sample mean could be one of a number of errors away from the true mean.

Any distribution will be skewed (positively or negatively) according to whether $p(\text{success})$ is near to 0 or near to 1.

So in the binomial distribution we see practically everything that has been explored so far. It is easier to see the concepts, because they can be calculated easily. In sampling, where there may be more than 2 outcomes per trial, the picture is too complex to visualize, and confidence in the underlying theory is reassuring.

Questions

1 It is believed that 32% of a population are active members of a library. Assuming this to be true, if 10 people are interviewed at random, calculate the probabilities that:

a) none of them
b) 7 of them
c) more than 2 of them

will be active members of a library.

2 A survey in a library showed that 7241 books out of 9821 sought were found by the readers without staff assistance.

a) What is the probability that any one book sought will be found by the reader without help?
b) If seven individual readers come to the library to look for seven different titles (one each), what are the probabilities that they will find:

a) all 7 titles
b) at least 2 titles?

3 The Fullharmonic Music Library claims an 87% success rate on requests for recorded music. Taking a random sample of 12 requests, calculate the probabilities that:

a) all 12 will be satisfied
b) 11 will be satisfied
c) at least 10 will be satisfied.

Chapter 10
Sampling

Summary

This chapter surveys various methods of sampling and links the
theory of probability with the practice of inference. After
reading this chapter you should have added to your understanding of probability and be more ready to approach the
following chapters on inference and testing, where the randomness of sampling and its implications needs to be understood.

Dedication

We feel that this chapter should be dedicated to the student who wrote in an
examination: ' "Sampling with replacement" is using samples, then if they are not
correct or do not seem to be working then you can try again till you think you have
the right answer.' If you don't see the joke, read on!

When designing a research project, one should start with a careful consideration
of what end results are hoped for, what it is that the investigator is trying to measure
or test.

The researcher is investigating an idea, not trying to prove anything. Designing a
project means setting up a situation from which answers may emerge. Great care
must be taken not to conduct a survey in such a way that certain answers are more
likely to emerge than others. This would introduce bias into a survey, and would
obviously affect the reliability and usefulness of the results. There is certain to be
some bias anyway, due to chance factors unavoidable in the selection of cases, but
chance can be measured probabilistically and allowed for.

Representativeness of samples

We take samples because it is often not possible to survey an entire population. The population is, in effect, being studied through the sample. Selection of a sample should therefore aim to reproduce the population on a small scale, in the incidence and variability of the characteristics being investigated. From what we can learn about the sample, we want to reach certain conclusions about the population. These conclusions can only be estimations, but for results to be reliable, and worth having at all, the representativeness of the sample is fundamental. If a sample is taken properly we can work out how good the estimates are.

Sample size

The desirable size of a sample does not necessarily reflect the size of the population from which it is drawn. A large population does not need to be measured by a large sample to give valid results. Validity depends more on the appropriateness of the questions asked, on the skill of the investigators, and on the fullness, accuracy and honesty of the responses. Of greater importance than sample size is the degree of accuracy required in the resulting sample statistics, i.e. how reliable they are to be as estimates of population parameters.

We may proceed on the basis that a 'large' sample of over 30 would be sufficient for most purposes. A sample of this size allows us to measure sample statistics against the standard normal distribution and estimate confidence levels on the grounds of probability.

Sampling frame

The population to be sampled can be limited and defined by some factor or factors: e.g. age, gender, occupation residence, income bracket. This is not to introduce a bias, as long as we intend to generalize only to a population limited by the same factors. The sample frame is the list of the entire population as defined, from which a sample is to be drawn. It may be an actual list, a telephone directory, an electoral register, a university's student records. They have their limits. A telephone directory excludes people without a phone, for instance. The growing practice of market research by random digit dialling has limits which must be recognized. In real situations, the 'list' may not in fact be written, and in many cases it would be impracticable to produce one.

Random selection of samples

Sampling theory is founded on randomness and probability. To allow probability to operate fully, samples should be chosen randomly. This means that:

a) each member of the population should have an equal chance of being chosen, and
b) every possible combination of N elements should have an equal chance of constituting the sample, including samples in which the same elements appear more than once.

Random numbers

The best method of random selection is to use a table of random numbers. These are computer-produced, or can be tediously assembled with a pocket calculator. There is no order to a random number table, but integers 0 to 9 occur with approximately equal frequency. They are random in that each digit has an equal probability of appearing in each position on the page. Tables are usually printed in columns of two or four, but they can be used singly, in pairs, or in any other grouping.

If you wished to sample 100 libraries out of a population of 400 libraries, the first step would be to number the libraries 1 to 400. Taking the random number table, choose a starting point, using some device like the day's date, or a pin. Using 20 September, go to the 20th line and start at the 9th digit. Pick out 100 3-digit numbers between 001 and 400, ignoring numbers above 400. These numbers indicate the libraries from the numbered list which are to constitute the sample.

Sampling with replacement (unrestricted random sampling)

Once a number has been picked, it is 'replaced', and is eligible to be picked again. Any library could therefore have its score counted more than once within the sample. This method is technically correct. Statisticians say this is the purest method, and some the only one to use.

Sampling without replacement

Sometimes it might be preferred to have 100 *unique* cases. In this case a number appearing a second time is passed over. This is called *sampling without replacement*, or *simple random sampling*. A researcher may not want to use a case more than once. If the sample is to be only a small one it would look silly if the same case appeared two or three times. Simple random sampling reduces the likelihood of a misleading or unrepresentative sample, and is said to produce more precise estimators of the population, but does not meet the second requirement of random sampling, that all possible combinations have an equal chance of appearing.

Sampling without replacement would give many millions of possible combinations of 100 out of 400, giving, one would think, a sufficient degree of randomness for most purposes. The possible combinations available when sampling *with* replacement are very much greater, since there are combinations in which an individual case could appear 1, 2, 3, . . . 100 times.

A sample randomly selected could, theoretically, come predominantly from one section of the population (given condition b) above). This would not matter much if the population were homogeneous, i.e. every section having the characteristic you are measuring in more or less the same proportions. One section would therefore almost exactly resemble any other and would show approximately the same mean and variance. Where a population is not homogeneous, or less than adequately so, the size of the *sampling error* (the difference between the sample mean and the population's true mean) could be large. (See later section on stratified sampling.)

Random selection could thus still produce a biased sample, but it does present a *method* of selection which is free from bias. Inferential statistical techniques take the chance factor into account, and allow us to calculate the confidence to be placed in a statistic derived from a sample.

Other sampling methods

Random sampling is fundamental to statistical inference. Unfortunately, it requires a knowledge of all the population elements to be reasonably sure of homogeneity, and this is not always possible.

When the population is small enough to list and can be ascertained (e.g. all the registered amateur football clubs in England and Wales, all the currently enrolled students in the Law Department, all readers who still have books out after 14 days) they can be numbered and a sample selected by means of random numbers.

Many investigations, especially sociological and economic ones, sample a population with far too many individual elements for this method to be possible. They cannot all be known, the population is fluid, and a complete listing would be impossible or too expensive. Some other technique of sampling, which still permits the random factor to operate in the selection of the sample, must be employed.

The multi-stage sample

A population is divided into a set of clusters (primary sampling units) and a simple random selection of clusters is taken. The resulting sample (the secondary sampling units) is similarly divided into clusters and the clusters subjected to a simple random selection. This process goes on as long as necessary, until the ultimate sampling units are isolated – these may be clusters or individual elements. Where whole clusters are surveyed, and individuals are not selected from them, this is more particularly known as *cluster sampling*. Numbers of cases drawn from each cluster should normally be proportionate to the number of individuals in the cluster.

Suppose we want to interview 1000 children about reading habits and library use. It would be legitimate to restrict the survey to registered library users if required, but we would want to eliminate biases like social class, type of school, parental influence, and similar factors, and let these occur in the final sample by chance. A possible procedure would be:

1   Number all the library authorities sequentially, but in no particular order;
2   Draw off a simple random sample;
3   Expand the list of authorities into a list of individual children's libraries, then take a sample as before;
4   From the individual libraries' registers of readers, take a random sample of children, who will then constitute the ultimate sampling units.

The method works best when the clusters in the primary sample are homogeneous with respect to the relevant variable, with the result that the ultimate sample is heterogeneous. This is good, as it approximates more closely to a simple random sample, and the sampling error of the sample is minimized. Sampling error is still generally greater from a multi-stage sample than from a simple random sample, and this has to be borne in mind when applying and interpreting tests of statistical significance. It may be necessary to apply more rigorous tests of hypotheses.

The stratified random sample

If we wanted to survey the involvement of academic library staff in teaching or professional activities outside the library, and we took a simple random sample of academic libraries, we might conceivably find that the sample consisted mostly or entirely of small libraries with a small number of staff. The size of a library's staff might well have an important effect on the ability of staff members to engage in extralibrary activities. A sample which excluded larger libraries would undoubtedly give misleading results.

A better method in a case like this would be to classify the libraries into several groups (strata) according to size – by numbers of staff, bookstock, or some other criterion. Libraries would be selected from each group in proportion to the size of the group. This ensures that each group is properly represented in the sample. Each stratum would be more likely to be homogeneous within itself, while heterogeneity is achieved by sampling all strata.

Proportionate stratified sampling

A sample of 20 libraries from a population of 100 should reflect the known balance, which might be 50 school libraries, 30 public libraries, 15 academic libraries and 5 special libraries. Sampling by proportions would give us 10 school libraries, 6 public, 3 academic and 1 special.

Disproportionate stratified sampling

The sample above would give only 1 special library – not enough data to determine the range of variation of the characteristic amongst special libraries. We may take all 5 special libraries as a subgroup. We may 'oversample' small categories. The decision will depend on whether we know or suspect that a variable is strongly related to a type of library, e.g. we may know that bookfunds are similar amongst school libraries and they vary considerably amongst special libraries. The sample could therefore have all 5 special libraries but only 6 of the school libraries.

Stratified sample methods are necessary when the population is not homogeneous, e.g. the population of a city, as this contains different age groups, different social and economic circumstances, racial areas, etc. It is also useful when it is desired to make comparisons between sub-populations (strata) of a population.

Stratification results in sub-populations that are homogeneous. If strata were formed by specifying 2 or more variables (e.g. by social class plus gender of the informant) they would be more homogeneous still. This is important, as homogeneity reduces the size of the sampling error. Stratified sampling controls the characteristics of the stratum, and eliminates the bias effect of that characteristic.

Generally, stratified sampling reduces sampling error against a simple random sample of the same size. This means that one has to make allowances in the interpretation of results, and use of the usual statistical formulae could be misleading unless one makes adjustments. Nevertheless, many of the results obtained from a stratified sample can be tested by elementary statistical techniques. Variables chosen for stratification must be related to the dependent and/or independent variables of the study. If unrelated variables are used (e.g. in the library study: colour of eyes, hat size) the strata will be no more homogeneous in relation to the criterion variables than the total population.

A drawback of this method is that you must have a list of the total population and enough information about each member on the list to divide the list into population sub-categories. If you intend to do a proportionate sample, you would want to know the distribution of the relevant variables. An example: if you know that 60% of the students in a department of library studies do the Business Elective, you would want 6 out of 10 students in your sample to be doing the Business Elective. Without this knowledge of the characteristics of the population, drawing off the correct proportions involves a certain amount of guesswork and, consequently, increased possibility of error.

It is possible to stratify after one has collected the data by simple random sampling and other methods. You might do this if observation of a survey results showed an imbalance of respondents, such as 3 males for every 8 females, more young than old, more black than white, etc.

Non-probability sampling methods

Samples which do not involve the concept of random selection should generally be avoided. Statistical inference and the carrying out of statistical tests depend on the measurable properties of probability; if this basis is abandoned, there is no basis for calculating sampling error, and conclusions must be suspect. Nevertheless, these techniques are widely used.

Systematic sampling and quasi-random sampling

Systematic sampling involves selecting names from a list. The starting point alone is chosen randomly, then every *n*th name is taken into the sample.

The lists commonly used are usually in some systematic order, whether it is by seniority, department, or street and house number order. Systematic sampling is therefore not comparable to random sampling. Categorization of a list might give names from certain categories a greater chance of being chosen, and so introduce an unacceptable bias.

If the list can be regarded as in a more or less random order, or names on the list are subjected to a randomizing process, or if the feature by which it is arranged is not related to the nature of the survey, the method of selection by a sampling fraction (every nth case) can be regarded as approximately equal to simple random sampling. This is referred to as *quasi-random sampling.* A purely alphabetical listing can be included here, since a name's position is determined solely by spelling, and its position predicates nothing about the characteristics possessed by the owner.

Systematic and quasi-random sampling clearly violate the principles that every case and every combination of cases should have an equal chance of being chosen. Once the starting point is fixed, if only every 10th case is chosen, the other 9s have no chance of being chosen. Also, only 1 sample of size n is possible from that starting point. Since there are only as many starting points as there are items in the list, the number of possible combinations is severely limited.

Quota sampling

This is a popular method. The interviewer is given a list of desirable characteristics and then has to find and interview a quota of people possessing those characteristics. In effect, the population is stratified by the chosen characteristics, such as age, gender, social class, occupation.

Bias and error are constant dangers, which can be reduced but not eliminated by careful instructions to interviewers. Human bias – the interviewer's choice about whom to approach – is inevitable. Another kind of weakness would be to interview people relaxing on a sunny Saturday afternoon in a city centre green area. Those not there because they are old, working, too busy shopping, watching a football match, or have seen enough of the city during the week, would not be represented. Interviewers might be instructed *where* to look for 'victims', e.g. specific addresses chosen by proper random methods.

Quota sampling, despite its defects, is considered to provide sufficiently representative results in surveys, unless a high degree of accuracy is essential. If very carefully done, reducing human bias sufficiently, it can give results similar to an equivalent stratified sample.

Voluntary samples

Subjects volunteer to take part in a study. This method is prone to bias, since the sample is self-selected, and volunteers may have personal reasons for taking part. A celebrated example is the Kinsey Report on the sexual behaviour of the human male, 1948, which used a voluntary sample of interviewees. Self-selected samples probably have too much in common to be heterogeneous in their responses.

Judgement sampling, or intuitive sampling

The interviewer may select what is, in his judgement, a random sample. This is too open to subjective bias to be of much use for statistical purposes. An interviewer may not approach certain people because they seem uncooperative, threatening, suspicious, in a hurry, or for other reasons unlikely to be useful.

Supplementary notes

Reducing the range of errors

If we want to reduce the possible range of errors in the sample mean (to within a narrower range of values of the variable) the standard error of the sampling distribution of means could be reduced by increasing sample size. This, however, would involve increasing the sample by four times, to reduce the standard error by only a half. For example, given a sample with $n = 100$ and $s = 5$, the *standard error of the mean* would be

$$s/\sqrt{n} = 5/\sqrt{100} = 0.5$$

but to reduce the standard error by half would require a sample of 400:

$$5/\sqrt{400} = 0.25$$

Finite population correction factor

In practice, most of the random sampling done is *simple* random sampling, without replacement, and is preferable in that it produces more accurate estimates of populations. The populations sampled, though they may be large, are finite in size. The Standard Normal Distribution (SND), one of the major probability distributions, extends to infinity, though in practice the table of the SND is taken to include all probabilities. In theory, however, the calculation of the *standard error of the mean* $(s/\sqrt{n})$ is based upon the assumption that the population is infinite, and that *unrestricted* random sampling is used. (The SND is introduced fully in the chapter on inference from sample to population.)

Where simple random sampling is employed, we should apply the finite population correction factor, which is $(1 - n/N)$, and calculate the standard error of the mean as

$$\frac{s}{\sqrt{n}} \times \sqrt{1 - \frac{n}{N}}$$

where n is the number in the sample, N is the number in the population, and s is the standard deviation of the sample data.

Whether we should use it or not depends on the size of the sample in relation to the population. At one extreme, if the whole population is surveyed, $(1 - n/N) = 0$, so it is inappropriate and can be ignored. If the sample is very small in relation to the population, e.g. 40 out of 200,000, the product of $(1 - n/N) = (1 - 40/200,000) = 0.9998$, so close to 1 that the difference can be ignored without much loss of accuracy in the results. As a general rule, the finite population correction factor can be ignored if the sample does not exceed 5% of the population. In many studies the size of the population may not be known, but common sense will usually tell us that it is big enough for a sample to be less than 5%.

It is hard for non-mathematicians to imagine why sampling a finite population would make much difference when randomness of choice seems wide enough. For instance, selecting 30 from a mere 1000 can be done in 2.4296 E 57 different ways, that is, the figure arrived at by moving the decimal point 57 places to the right! This is surely 'infinite' enough for all practical purposes? However, mathematicians and purists *do* argue in favour of the correction factor.

Part 4
Inference

Chapter 11
Inference from sample to population

Summary

In this chapter you meet two very important probability distributions, the Standard Normal Distribution (z-table) and the related t distribution, and see them applied to constructing confidence intervals for sample means. After studying this chapter, you should have a good appreciation of these distributions and have a sound foundation for following with ease the remaining chapters on inference and hypothesis testing.

Making inferences about populations from the evidence of samples, and testing hypotheses by means of samples, requires reference to a probability distribution as a means of estimating confidence in the statistics resulting from the tests. A distribution heavily used is the Standard Normal Distribution. This is available in the form of a table of 'areas under the normal curve', more usually called the z-table.

The standard normal distribution

We will appreciate how this abstract model relates to concrete examples of research, and see its application to one question – the estimation of a confidence interval for a sample mean. The SND will be considered at some length, because an understanding of it is fundamental to so much of statistical inference.

The z-table is reproduced in Appendix 2. The SND is a mathematical abstraction and does not refer to any population or variable in particular. It refers to a symmetrical 'bell-shaped' curve, and measures areas under the curve at many points. In theory it is a histogram of an infinite number of points, while in fact the table plots the probability values of a selection – a large selection – of points along the axis. This means that there are values even in the spaces between figures, but it is not practicable to show these.

The SND assumes an infinite population, which is why the curve is drawn with the ends left open, but almost 100% of the area under the curve is covered by the figures on the *z*-table. The mean of the SND is 0 (as in any distribution $\Sigma (x - \bar{x}) = 0$). It is stepped off in *standard deviations* from the mean, each standard deviation having the value of 1. Tables usually stretch from −3.49sd to +3.49sd, or from a theoretical minus-infinity to a theoretical plus-infinity. Between the limits stated lies 99.96% of the theoretical population. The notional extension beyond these limits to infinity therefore accounts for only 0.04%.

The importance of these facts lies in knowing that the figures in the SND represent probabilities, not frequencies as in the more usual histograms and curves that we have met.

The column headed *z* shows standard deviations in tenths, spreading away from the mean (μ). The columns headed 0.00, 0.01, etc., give ten divisions of each tenth of a standard deviation, so allowing two decimal places of standard deviation. The top line, for example, shows −3.4, −3.41, −3.42, etc. standard deviations.

Hold the table so that the *z*-column is horizontal. The mean of the curve is the space between the two central rows (now columns) of figures. While standard deviations are counted from the mean outwards, the figures indicating probabilities read from the left, notional zero, to the right, notional 1. Figures increase slowly at first, then more rapidly up to the mean, then decline in proportion towards the top end of the table. This is analogous to a frequency distribution where (whether symmetrical or not doesn't matter at the moment) the height of the curve is determined by frequencies, and shows a rise and fall.

It can help to think of the figures as showing steps in the gradual 'shading in' of the area under the curve. If each figure shows how much has been shaded, then it also shows the probability that a figure randomly chosen would come from within that area.

Some examples:

What are the probabilities

1   that a figure would be one of those below the mean? The probability is 0.5.
2   that a figure would be one of those between +1 sd and −1.55 sd? Refer to the table at these sd points. The top figure is 0.8413, the lower one 0.0606. The area between them is therefore 0.8413 − 0.0606 = 0.7807.

The answers to these questions give the *probability densities* of the areas specified, i.e. the probabilities that a randomly-chosen member of a population would have a value in those areas.

Standard units

To take us a step nearer to appreciating the use of the SND in hypothesis testing when dealing with named variables, we need to understand the idea of a standard unit. Populations and variables studied by researchers differ greatly between themselves, but hypothesis testing depends on reducing actual figures to equivalent neutral z-scores, to see how they fit the concept of the model SND. How they fit makes it possible to make statements about sample statistics, based on probabilities.

Suppose a population of, for instance, the number of newspapers bought over a period, with a mean of 65 and a standard deviation of 6.1. What are the probabilities that a randomly-chosen member of the population would give a score of

a) 72 or less?
b) greater than 61?

Any score on the variable is a distance from the mean. That distance can be measured by simple subtraction. The distance is expressible as the number of times the standard deviation will divide into it. The final answer is a number of standard deviations, therefore a value of z. To calculate a standard unit we use the formula:

$$z = \frac{\bar{x} - \mu}{\sigma}$$

which in the case of a) means $\dfrac{72(\bar{x}) - 65(\mu)}{6.1(\sigma)} = \dfrac{7}{6.1} = 1.1475z \ (1.15)$

Refer to the z-table and confirm that z at 1.15 sd has the figure 0.8749. This shows the amount of the area under the curve 'shaded' from the zero-end of the curve. It shows also the probability density of the area. The probability that a random score would be 72 or less is 0.8749 or 87.49%.

A similar calculation for 61 gives:

$$z + \frac{61 - 65}{6.1} = \frac{-4}{6.1} = -0.6557z \ (0.66)$$

From the z-table, −0.66 sd gives 0.2546. Since this is the probability up to 61, and we want the probability of over 61, subtract 0.2546 from 1, and $1 - 0.2546 = 0.7454$ or 74.54%.

The SND is in essence a table of 'errors'. Since not all figures are equal to the mean of 0, they vary from the mean by greater or lesser errors. Jumping forward a few steps, we will want to apply this fact of error to down-to-earth questions such as: 'The mean age of a sample of my library's users is 42.8 years; how different is that from the true mean age of *all* my library's users?'

One last look at the z-table before we move on. Researchers are commonly only interested in a very few values of z, and a very few proportions of the area under the curve. This statement may seem to make most of the foregoing explanation redundant, but in fact does not.

Many hypothesis tests look at the regions showing 95% and 99% of the area under the curve, spread evenly, centrally either side of the mean μ. For 95% this means that the area under the curve is divided into probability densities of:

0.025	0.95	0.025
z	μ	z

The two points z represent probability densities of 0.025 and 0.975, since densities build up from left to right. Look at the z-table to find the figures closest to 0.025 and 0.975. As it happens they are both there, at $-1.96z$ and $+1.96z$. We can say then that the central 95% of the area under the curve lies between ±1.96 standard deviations. A random case has thus a 95% probability of having a value within ±1.96sd from the mean.

For 99% the same reasoning applies. The areas under the curve, building up from left to right, are:

0.005	0.99	0.005
z	μ	z

The two densities at z are therefore 0.005 and 0.995. Finding the nearest figures is not so obvious, as the nearest figures are at -2.57 and -2.58, and similarly at the high end. The exact values lie between these pairs (the space between columns has hidden values), so the true positions of 0.005 and 0.995 are ±2.575 (see also Figure 11.1). Some texts are less precise, and settle for 2.58, which is not unreasonable. In this text 2.575 will be used.

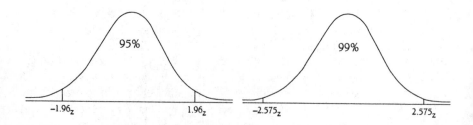

Fig. 11.1   Standard normal distribution

The SND has been studied at this length because it is vital to much that is about to follow. Having now arrived at least at an intuitive grasp, all that follows from the nature of the SND is comparatively uncomplicated.

The first really useful application of the z-table that we shall consider is how to evaluate a sample mean as an estimator of the true population mean.

Confidence intervals for large sample means

Inferential statistical processes allow us to make statements about a population from the evidence of a sample. Can the sample statistics be generalized to the population, i.e. does the sample give a reliable picture of how the measured variable is distributed in the population at large? We cannot be certain, but conclusions can be reached with a level of *confidence*, which is related to the known *probabilities* involved.

It has been stated that the SND is a distribution of errors. From the shape of the curve and figures in the *z*-table it is obvious that there many more *small* errors (68.26 lie within only ±1 sd) than there are *large* errors (only 1% lie outside ±2.575 sd). So it follows that a sample mean is more likely to be close to the true population mean than very different from it.

If all the large samples of a given size were taken, and their means plotted on the same axis as the population distribution, we would have a curve of means known as the *sampling distribution of the means*. It is the smaller one in Figure 11.2. This is normally-distributed around the mean of the population, i.e. it has the same properties and proportions as the SND.

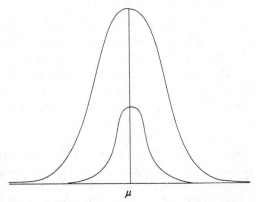

μ

Fig. 11.2 Standard normal distribution and sampling distribution of the means

The sampling distribution of means has its own standard deviation (called the *standard error* (SE)) which is smaller than the population standard deviation and that of the sample. It has the same properties and probabilities as the SD.

A single sample mean is one of very many sample means constituting this sampling distribution, so we can say with confidence that there is a high probability that it is closely similar to the mean of the distribution (which is the mean of the population). Statistics users will normally state the level of confidence required, commonly 95% or 99%, so it could be said that one is 95% confident that a sample

mean lies within 1.96 standard errors, plus and minus, of the population mean –
because we know that 95% of means lie within those limits.

With that same level of confidence the statistics from our one sample can be used
to estimate the standard error of the sampling distribution. (See the Central Limit
Theorem later in chapter). The standard error is calculated from:

$$\frac{s}{\sqrt{n}}$$

i.e. the standard deviation of the sample over the square root of the number of cases
in the sample.

A sample of 300 scores on an IQ test, with a mean of 109.9 and a standard
deviation of 11.1 would yield a standard error of

$$\frac{11.1}{\sqrt{300}} = 0.641$$

Now consider the following. If we could assume that the sample mean is the same
as the true population mean, we could extend it by ±1.96 standard errors (1.96 ×
0.641 = 1.256), i.e.

$$\bar{x} \pm (1.96 \times SE) = 109.9 \pm 1.256$$

which would give us an interval of IQ scores from 108.644....111.156.

Under this assumption, we could say that 95% of the sample means would have
a value between 108.644 and 111.156 IQ scores, and none of them would be more
than 1.256 scores from the population mean score.

We don't know what the true mean score is, of course, but now we know the
standard error and can use it as an estimate of the standard error of the sampling
distribution of means, we can assert that 95% of all means lie within $\mu \pm (1.96 \times SE)$,
i.e. −1.256-------μ------- +1.256.

Another unknown is, where does our sample mean stand relative to the
population μ? Our sample mean of 109.9 is extended to 108.644 ------ 111.156, but
the sample mean could be as much as 1.96 SE above or below the true mean and the
true mean would still be within the interval of 108.644 and 111.156.

$$
\begin{array}{ccc}
 & 108.644 & 111.156 \\
(\text{if } \bar{x} = \mu) & \vdash\!\!-\!\!-\!\!-\ 109.9\ -\!\!-\!\!-\!\!\dashv & \\
 & \ \ \vdash\ 109.9\ \dashv & (\text{if } \bar{x} \neq \mu) \\
108.644 & 111.156 &
\end{array}
$$

This extension of the sample mean from being a *point estimate* to being an *interval
estimate* is called a *confidence interval* (CI). It allows us to say we are 95% confident
that the true mean is somewhere between the limit values, and that our sample mean
is no more than 1.256 score marks (= 1.96 × SE) 'out' from the true mean. In saying

this, we accept a 5% chance that the true mean is *outside* our interval.

The formula for a confidence interval is:

$$95\%CI = \bar{x} \pm (1.96 \times \frac{s}{\sqrt{n}})$$

For a 99% confidence interval, substitute 2.575z for 1.96z. Using the IQ example, the confidence interval for the sample mean is

$$109.9 \pm (1.96 \times \frac{11.1}{\sqrt{300}}) = 109.9 \pm 1.256$$

Subtracting and adding 1.256 gives us the interval:

$$108.644 < \mu < 111.156.$$

IQ scores are usually given as integers, so the fractions can give a false sense of accuracy and it would be sensible to round them to 109 and 111.

Having done all this, we are only 95% confident of the position of the true mean. There remains a 5% probability that our sample mean was *not* one of the central 95% and that the true mean lies *outside* our interval.

The Central Limit Theorem

If a population is normally-distributed, then the sampling distribution of means will also be normally-distributed. Mathematicians assure us that the standard error of the sampling distribution can be approximated from the standard deviation and number of a single sample.

The Central Limit Theorem states that even if the parent population is *not* normally-distributed, a sampling distribution of means for large samples (= more than 30) would still be approximately normal, so again the sample statistics can be used to estimate the standard error of the sampling distribution of means.

The theorem means that we don't need to ask whether the parent population is normally-distributed or not, as long as we use large samples.

Small samples: the use of the *t*-distribution

We need to become acquainted with the *t*-distribution, a probability distribution closely associated with the *z*-distribution. A partial table, showing figures for alpha (α) = 0.05 and 0.01, is reproduced in Appendix 2.

As seen above, when samples are large we can make the assumption that the sampling distribution of means is normally-distributed, for samples of a given size from the population. The standard error of the sampling distribution is $\sigma/\sqrt{n}$, where σ is the standard deviation of the parent population. In most cases σ is unknown, so an approximation is obtained using the standard deviation of the sample, i.e. $s/\sqrt{n}$.

The *t*-distribution is a family of distributions of sample means. While the *z*-table shows distributions as if the population σ were known, the *t*-table shows what distributions would look like when population σ is unknown. It is calculated from:

$$\frac{\bar{x} - \mu}{s/\sqrt{n}}$$

for different sizes of sample, that is, for all degrees of freedom to infinity. There is a different distribution for each degree of freedom (df). (See paragraph on degrees of freedom later in chapter.)

Look, for example, at the column headed $t.025$, which shows the number of standard errors enclosing 95% of the distribution of means. Where a sample size is very small, a 95% confidence interval would be very wide. As sample sizes increase (in terms of degrees of freedom) so the width of a confidence interval reduces. Where the sample is big enough for degrees of freedom to be infinite, the figures at the bottom of the columns are seen to be those of the standard normal distribution. The t-distribution based on $s/\sqrt{n}$ becomes the same as the z-distribution, based on $\sigma/\sqrt{n}$.

Sample size

It is widely accepted that a sample of over 30 is enough to be regarded as a large sample, and the z-distribution is used, while a sample of 30 and fewer is regarded as a small sample, and the t-table is used.

To be really pedantic, the sample size at which degrees of freedom becomes infinite is not 31, as might be inferred from the table, but over 120. Many statisticians accept, however, that the differences in the critical values between $n = 31$ and $n = 120$ are so small that they won't seriously affect results, and that therefore '$n = 31+$' can be regarded as a 'large' sample.

One limitation on the use of the t-table must be noted. For reasons which need not be gone into here (they are well explained by Blalock; see bibliography) it is necessary to be able to assume that the parent population is itself normally-distributed. Where degrees of freedom are infinite, this assumption is not necessary. Where there is any doubt, if possible make sure your sample has more than 30 cases!

Degrees of freedom

This is an important concept in probability and is related to the randomness of sampling. It implies that all cases in a sample are freely chosen, except the last one. A series of figures 17, 13, 9, 21, 8, 18, and (5), have a mean of 13. All figures except the one in brackets were free to be any value. The one in brackets is not free, it *must* be the figure that will give the mean of 13. The degrees of freedom here are $7 - 1$, and the degree of freedom is generalized as $n - 1$. Note that it doesn't matter which figure is regarded as the 'last', or that the mean is not usually known in advance. The principle is commonsense enough. As stated above, in large samples the degree of freedom is infinite, but with small samples notice has to be taken of it, as in the following example.

Confidence intervals for small samples

The procedure is the same as that for large samples, except that one must use the value of t appropriate to the sample size. The selective t-table printed in this text has four columns, plus two listing degrees of freedom. The second, headed $t.025$, and the fourth, headed $t.005$, are for estimating 95% and 99% confidence intervals respectively.

A promotion test is tried out on 12 junior managers, before wider application. The mean score was 110 points, with $s = 11.2$.

A 95% confidence interval is:

$$\bar{x} \pm (t \times \frac{s}{\sqrt{n}})$$

Degrees of freedom is determined by $n - 1$, in this case $12-1 = 11$. The corresponding value of t (from the $t.025$ column), is 2.201.

$$110 \pm (2.201 \times \frac{11.2}{\sqrt{12}}) = 110 =- 7.116$$

which gives a confidence interval of $102.88 < \mu < 117.116$

Questions

1 50 students reported the time spent (in hours per week) in a college library. The sample data showed a mean time of 9.8 hours, with a standard deviation of 4.3 hours. Construct a 95% confidence interval for the mean time.
2 An insurance company noted the numbers of car-theft-related claims received by themselves and other companies over 75 randomly selected days from a 5-year period. The sample data had a mean of 35.9 claims, with a standard deviation of 21.85 claims. Construct a 99% confidence interval for the mean number of claims.
3 Over a period, a mobile library made experimental stops in a village off the normal route. After 25 visits, the mean attendance was found to be 13 visitors, with a standard deviation of 1.8. Construct a 95% confidence interval for the expected number of users if the service were to be implemented regularly.

Chapter 12
Introduction to hypothesis testing

Summary

In this and following chapters we see how hypotheses are tested by the taking of samples. The difference between a hypothesized statistic and the sample statistic is tested for statistical significance, that is, does the sample support the hypothesis or cause us to reject it? Tests are commonly applied to belief in a population mean, to the similarity of means of two populations, and to proportions. Here we see significance testing for a single mean.

Elements of hypothesis testing

Hypothesis tests, or tests for statistical significance, require a number of elements. These can be introduced by an example using concepts that can be seen intuitively. We can then move on to examples where we must put our trust in the laws of probability and in the theoretical distributions which are used as testing tools.

A gambler claims that he has a secret method of picking out a named card from a group placed face down on a table. Unlikely as this claim seems, a club owner puts the claim to the test.

a) There is a *theory*, that the gambler is only guessing, and that if he gets it right it will only be by luck.
b) There is a *challenge* – the gambler is not guessing, he really has a method and will prove it.
c) A *test* is agreed. He is allowed four attempts to pick out a specified card from five placed face down, and must achieve this all four times.
d) There is a *distribution of probabilities* of success. From the chapter on probability, recall that the probability of success at the first trial is 1/5. The probability

of getting it right twice is $1/5 \times 1/5 = 1/25$. The full distribution of Pass and Fail for the test is:

		1st trial	2nd trial	3rd trial	4th trial
Correct choice	1	P	F		
	2	P	P	F	
	3	P	P	P	F
	4	P	P	P	P

Probabilities of

$$1 = \frac{1}{5}$$

$$2 = \frac{1}{5} \times \frac{1}{5} = \frac{1}{25}$$

$$3 = \frac{1}{5} \times \frac{1}{5} \times \frac{1}{5} = \frac{1}{125}$$

$$4 = \frac{1}{5} \times \frac{1}{5} \times \frac{1}{5} \times \frac{1}{5} = \frac{1}{625}$$

The probabilities of failing rapidly increase with each trial

$$(\frac{4}{5}, \frac{24}{25}, \frac{124}{125}, \frac{624}{625}).$$

Each trial completed successfully therefore strengthens belief that he actually can do what he claims.

e) There has to be a *point of decision* taken from the distribution of probabilities. The club owner decrees four trials only, and success at odds of 1 in 625 are convincing.

f) A *decision* will be made to retain or reject the theory that is being tested. If the point of decision is passed, the owner accepts that the probability that the gambler really *has* a method is stronger than the probability that he is bluffing.

g) A *risk*. The decision is made, but the possibility remains that the gambler may have been bluffing, and has just been extremely lucky to have passed the test.

Note that the definition of the test is arbitrary. It falls to the investigator to determine how 'hard' a test will be, i.e. what level of success is necessary to be convincing, given the probabilities involved. If testing a new drug, it would not be good enough to be confident that it would probably only kill 1 in 625!

Terms

The proper terminology must now be introduced.

Null hypothesis

A claim is made, a belief expressed, a statistic is held to be the norm, e.g. the average rent paid by students for accommodation is £45 per week. A single sample may show a mean of, say, £42 per week, but the belief in £45 is still asserted. Any difference is seen as due merely to chance in the composition of the sample, and there is no (null) significant difference from the hypothesized figure. The club owner confidently asserts that the gambler can't possibly see the value of a face-down card.

Alternative hypothesis

The null hypothesis is challenged. Experience may suggest that the average rental is significantly more (or less) than £45. Or one could simply say 'it is not £45'. Our hero asserts that he is not bluffing – he really has the skill claimed.

A test

In the cards example the test is a practical one: 'Let's see you do it'. Normally we will be concerned with randomly-composed samples. Either way, the interest lies in seeing whether the test produces a result that confirms the null hypothesis.

A test requires parameters: a *distribution* of probabilities to be a model against which the test can be compared; *a critical value*, a cut-off point on the distribution on which a decision to accept or reject the null hypothesis will be made; a stated *number of trials* (a sample is just a number of 'trials').

Distribution

Our test used a simple, predictable, distribution

$$\frac{1}{5}, \frac{1}{25}, \frac{1}{125}, \frac{1}{625}, \frac{1}{3125}, \frac{1}{15625} \ ... \ \text{etc.}$$

The distributions we normally use are theoretically more complicated.

Critical value

This is the chosen limit of 'chance'. The gambler is only guessing. Any 'successes' are due only to chance, to sheer luck, and the null hypothesis still holds, provided that the successes remain within the critical value (CV). If the gambler's successes pass the CV, however, they would indicate more than luck, and encourage one to accept that he really does have the skill.

The CV of 1/625 was chosen in this test. The gambler 'passed' the CV, and moved on to what could have been a fifth trial.

Decision

Having set the parameters of the test, the investigator has to decide what to make of the result. Sensibly, he will accept it. If he is not happy, another and more rigorous test can be done.

The club owner said, 'I'll believe him if he can get it right four times.' Another might have insisted on six times. If the gambler had passed either test, the challenger would normally accept the result, and reject his own null hypothesis.

Confidence level

The critical value determines the level of confidence which one can have in the result of a test. 'I want to be 95% confident'. 'I must be 1/625 confident'. The decision to accept or reject a result is qualified as being *at the chosen level of confidence.* The risk remains that the gambler could have been bluffing all along and was just remarkably lucky! In the kinds of hypothesis testing that we will do here, confidence levels are expressed as percentages, commonly 95% and 99%.

From this preliminary survey, we can now turn to more realistic examples of hypothesis testing.

Significance tests: one mean

The testing of various types of hypothesis by statistical methods involves the application of a small group of theoretical factors. These factors we have been studying and have applied some of them in the construction of confidence intervals. We will see that the underlying logic is very similar though the test situations differ.

In calculating confidence intervals we have used the Standard Normal Distribution (the z-table) and the t-distribution, and have seen the relationships between these tables. For a while we shall be concentrating on the SND.

The SND represents densities of probabilities between particular values of z. For instance, as we know, between $-1.96z$ and $+1.96z$ lies 95% of the area under the normal curve, equally distributed around the mean.

If we are looking at a normally-distributed *sampling distribution of means* from a population, we know from working with confidence intervals that we can state three principles with confidence:

1   95% of the sample means will have values within the range of $\mu \pm 1.96$ standard errors;

2   one random sample mean $\bar{x}$ from the population has a 95% chance of coming from within that range;

3   95% of the sample means would include the population mean μ within their 95% confidence intervals, and 5% would not.

These ideas can be taken further and applied to a hypothesis, e.g. the belief that the mean value of a variable in a population is a specific figure. If the population mean

μ is believed to be (say, for the sake of a figure) 64, then the mean of any random sample drawn from that population will be one of the means in the *sampling distribution of means*, which has a mean of 64. As the sampling distribution of means is normally-distributed, we can apply the attributes of the SND to the sampling distribution.

From what has been reviewed above, we can be sure that 95% of means will have values within the range of 64 ± 1.96 standard errors. Provided that a single sample mean is a value within that range, we continue to hold that $\mu = 64$, and accept that if the *sample* mean is not also 64 the difference is simply due to chance in the random selection of the sample.

If $\bar{x}$ falls outside the 95% range, i.e. more than 1.96 standard errors from μ, there are two possible conclusions.

1   The sample mean is untypical, one of those only likely to occur with a probability of 5%, but it is nevertheless one from the sampling distribution of means whose $\mu = 64$.

2   A mean outside the 95% range has only a low probability of occurring; since it has occurred, the hypothetical mean of 64 may not be true after all.

The reasoning behind conclusion 2 is simple. See the diagram below.

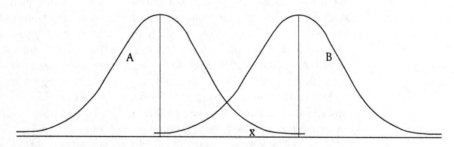

Fig. 12.1   Sample means – populations A and B

Any sample mean will more probably come from the area close to its population mean than from further away. If a sample thought to be drawn from population A has a mean which is *not* close to the μ of population A (an event with a low probability), then perhaps it comes from population B, and is close to the mean of *that* population.

The concepts 'close' and 'further away' are ill-defined. A *critical value* is chosen to give a definite threshold.

Testing for the significance of a single mean

A hypothesis is a belief, a claim, a standard by which work is done.

A null hypothesis

For example, it is believed that the mean time taken to catalogue a book in an academic library is 15 minutes. If a sample should show a different mean time, this would be imputed to chance in the sampling, and would not alter the original belief. This is the hypothesized mean μ.

An alternative hypothesis

Suppose doubts have arisen in the librarian's mind. An alternative belief could take one of these forms:

'The mean is not 15 minutes'   it is $\neq$ 15 minutes
'It is a longer time'   it is > 15
'It is a shorter time'   it is < 15

For this exercise we are going to propose that the time is $\neq$ 15, i.e. if uncertain whether it is greater or less, test to see if it is 'different'.

A sample

This is taken to test the validity of the null hypothesis, and will have its own mean time and standard deviation, which have to be determined. For example, we will assume a sample where $n = 35$, $= \bar{x}$ 17 minutes, and $s = 5$ minutes.

A test

The parameters of the test must be set, using familiar concepts. Study Figure 12.2.

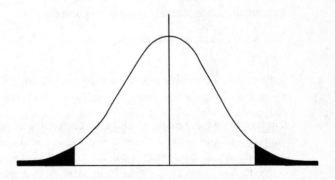

Fig. 12.2   Distribution of sample means where $\mu = 15$

If the population mean is truly 15 minutes, then any sample taken is one of those composing the theoretical sampling distribution of means whose μ is 15 minutes. A single sample mean $\bar{x}$ may vary from 15 provided that the value stays within the white area. If it is outside the white area, i.e. within either of the shaded areas, the difference is deemed to be too great to put down to sampling chance and is *statistically significant*. In this event, the hypothesized mean would be rejected. These areas and their boundaries have to be quantified.

It is usual to define the shaded areas first. These together form the *zone of rejection*, the area beyond the critical value, the area of risk, i.e. the risk of wrongly rejecting the null hypothesis. It is called alpha α. For this exercise we set the alpha level at 0.05. This means that the white area includes 95% of the means, and we would expect a single sample mean to be within that area with a probability of 95%.

The *critical value* which is the threshold between the areas of acceptance and rejection follows from the chosen alternative hypothesis (not equal to) and the chosen α level (0.05). It has to be (in this instance) $\pm$ 1.96 standard errors of the sampling distribution of means. This standard error is (as seen with confidence intervals) calculated from the statistics of the sample.

The test will measure how far apart are the hypothesized mean and the sample mean, and determine how many standard errors this distance represents. If the answer is less than or equal to 1.96, the hypothesized mean is retained. If it is greater than 1.96, the hypothesized mean will be rejected.

The test employs the formula:

$$z = \frac{\bar{x} - \mu}{\frac{s}{\sqrt{n}}}$$

where $\bar{x}$ is the sample mean, μ is the hypothesized mean of the population, and $s/\sqrt{n}$ is the standard error of the sampling distribution.

The difference between the two means is divided by the standard error of the sampling distribution – estimated from the sample – expressing the result as a number of standard errors (z-values). For example:

$$z = \frac{17 - 15}{\frac{5}{\sqrt{35}}} = 2.366 \; (2.37)$$

Decision

The calculated difference could have been as much as 1.96 standard errors away from $\mu = 15$ and belief in the null hypothesis could remain. The difference has now been shown to be greater than the critical value, so we must *reject* the null hypothesis. It takes longer than 15 minutes on average to catalogue a book.

Cautions

1   We cannot on this evidence say what the greater mean time in fact is, only that it is greater than 15 minutes.

2   We can only make this rejection with 95% confidence. There is still a 5% probability that the true time really is 15 minutes, and we are making a mistake in rejecting it.

3   The difference between 15 and 17 is said to be *statistically* significant. This is not the same as declaring that it is significant – it is only probably so in the terms of this test.

Summary

When you are tackling a question like this (whatever test is involved) it is advisable to 'set out your stall' and show the nature and parameters of your test. It will help clarify your decision. Summarizing the example worked out above:

1   State the null hypothesis: $H_0 : \mu = 15$ minutes.
2   State the alternative: $H_1 : \mu \neq 15$ minutes.
3   Choose α-level (0.05) and its appropriate critical value of z from the z-table ($\pm$ 1.96).
4   Take a sample and calculate $\bar{x}$ and s. In this example the figures are supplied.
5   Apply the test and calculate the test statistic for

$$\frac{\bar{x} - \mu}{\text{SE}}$$

6   Decide whether H_0 is to be accepted or rejected.

Your decision should be stated something like this: 'Because the test statistic is less than/greater than the critical value we accept/reject the null hypothesis at the n% level of confidence'. Personalize this to the question by adding, for example: 'The average time taken to catalogue a book is significantly greater than 15 minutes'.

Two-tailed and one-tailed tests

The above example shows a test conducted as a *two-tailed test*, because the difference could in the event have been significantly greater than or less than the H_0 figure. Either result would have been of interest to the investigator. Remember that in practice the nature of the test should ideally be decided *before* a sample is taken, otherwise the sample might determine the form of your question, rather than testing it.

The alternative hypothesis might have declared that the mean time is thought to be significantly greater than 15 minutes, and there is only cause for concern if this is shown to be the case. The decision to reject $\mu = 15$ would only be made if the test statistic were significantly *higher* than the critical value. The critical region would therefore be placed all on one side.

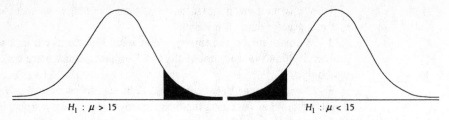

$H_1 : \mu > 15$ $H_1 : \mu < 15$

Fig. 12.3   Comparison between μ when greater and less than 15

The critical value of z for $\alpha = 0.05$ in such a *one-tailed test* will be 1.645.

If the alternative hypothesis is stated as $\mu < 15$ minutes, the critical value would be $- 1.645$.

Varying the test parameters

Note that the test statistic for the difference between hypothesized μ and the sample mean is a constant. Alpha could be set at any level (though 0.05 or 0.01 are most common). A test can be conducted at either level and as either a one-tailed or two-tailed test.

Decisions based upon the test statistic can differ according to the alpha level chosen and the form of test. Consider this:

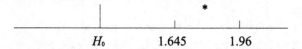

H_0 1.645   1.96

The asterisk represents a calculated test statistic. In a one-tailed test (critical value = 1.645), H_0 would be rejected; in a two-tailed test (critical value = 1.96) it would be retained.

Find and mark the following points on your z-table:

$\alpha = 0.05$
two-tailed test, $z = 1.96$, plus and minus
one-tailed test, $z = 1.645$, plus or minus

$\alpha = 0.01$
two-tailed test, $z = 2.575$, plus and minus
one-tailed test, $z = 2.33$, plus or minus

Errors in decisions

As we have seen, decisions are based on the probabilities, and the true state of affairs cannot be known without measuring the whole population. (In the cataloguing example, what is the population? We might be near the truth if we noted and averaged the times of cataloguing all books in one year, taking that as the population.)

a) In the worked example above, we believed that the mean time was 15 minutes, but rejected this on the basis of the test. We recognized, however, that 15 minutes might indeed *be* the true time and our rejection of it could have been a mistake.

b) Another possibility exists. Suppose the true mean time is indeed greater than 15 minutes (maybe 17, or thereabouts) but our test confirms our belief in the hypothesis that $\mu = 15$? We would continue to accept the lower figure, and be wrong for a different reason.

In the first place, we might be wrongly rejecting the true figure. In the second place, we would be wrongly accepting a false figure.

Table 12.1 summarizes this:

Table 12.1

	Accept H_0	Reject H_0
H_0 is true	Correct decision	Type I error
H_0 is false	Type II error	Correct decision

A Type I error is designated α
A type II error is designated β

We are concerned with Type I errors.

Questions

1 A photocopying machine is uneconomical unless it produces an average of 70 copies per working day. The reference librarian claims that it reaches this target, but the chief librarian is sceptical, and takes a random check of 40 days' use of the machine. He finds the mean to be only 66 copies per day, with a standard deviation of 7 copies. What can he conclude at the 99% level of confidence?

2 A children's librarian believes, from her observations, that the mean daily attendance over a year was 130. A random sample of 32 days' records showed a mean attendance of 121.5, with a standard deviation of 40.8. Does this mean that attendances do *not* average 130? Test her belief, with $\alpha = 0.05$, and interpret your result.

3 The Blackbury User Survey showed that the average age of Blackbury central library users, from a sample of 237, was 42.9 years, with a standard deviation of 14.03 years. A national survey of users of central libraries claims that the average age of users is 37 years 6 months. Test, with $\alpha = 0.05$, whether the Blackbury data support the claimed figure.

Chapter 13
Two-means tests

Summary

Using techniques already met, we consider tests for examining whether two populations are similar, that is, whether a variable has a similar distribution in the two populations. We see how to measure the significance of the difference between two means.

The previous chapter described the process of testing for the significance of a single sample mean against a null hypothesis. Two-means testing can be described more briefly. While the situations are different from those needing a one-mean test, the logic and procedures of the test are very similar.

Everyday life produces many occasions for comparisons:

- Will two similar cars of different makes have the same mean rate of petrol consumption?
- A library system uses two methods of book processing in its branches – are they equally efficient?
- Two geographical areas are similar in population, residential/industrial mix, and other characteristics. Is library use the same in both areas?
- If flocks of two breeds of sheep are fed the same diet, would they show the same average weight or wool yield?

The argument is that two 'populations' might be supposed to be similar with respect to a given characteristic. For example, our two flocks of sheep could be expected to have the same average weight and the same variability of weights (i.e. similar standard deviations), given that breeding conditions for both flocks are comparable. All the samples from a population would be matched by a corresponding set of samples in the other.

In practice, to test the theory, *one* random sample would be taken from *each* population. There is immediately the classic hypothesis test situation. As random samples may not normally show the same mean, is the difference between them due merely to sampling chance, or is it statistically significant? In plain language, a group from one flock should weigh the same as a group from the other flock, with a similar range of weights from lowest to highest, and the same average weight. The sample measurements would not be expected to be exactly the same, but not *very* different either, and the differences would be only due to sampling chance. How big a difference can be accepted which will still let us believe the flocks are the same in respect of weight? Again, this calls for a definite measure of difference – a critical value – which will help us decide the similarity or difference of the two flocks.

The null hypothesis for this kind of test is:

$H_0 : \mu_1 = \mu_2$

or as it could be expressed:

$H_0 : \mu_1 - \mu_2 = 0$

The alternative hypotheses are as before:

$H_1 : \mu_1 \neq \mu_2$
$H_1 : \mu_1 < \mu_2$
$H_1 : \mu_1 > \mu_2$

The theory

The theoretical basis of two-means tests begins with an assumption that two populations do in fact possess a characteristic in the same measure, and a test will confirm or overturn that assumption. Consider hypothetically some ideas that follow from this assumption.

1   Take a single population, and draw off all possible large samples of a given size, and calculate the means. A frequency curve of these means is the *sampling distribution of means*.

2   If all *pairs* of means are now taken, and one subtracted from the other in each pair, the *differences* could be plotted into a frequency curve, called the *sampling distribution of the differences between means*. This distribution would be normal in shape and would have a mean of zero and, of course, a standard error.

3   If it is true that two populations are the same, then the sampling distribution of means of each population would resemble each other. Step 2 could be carried out, this time taking each mean of population 2 from each mean of population 1. The resulting sampling distribution of differences would be the same as the one drawn from differences between means of *one* population. The mean difference would = 0, but two random samples drawn from two populations as though from one would usually show some difference.

Application of the theory

Differences between pairs of means from the distribution of means of a single population would mostly be small, given the nature of a normally-shaped distribution. Likewise, if a pair of samples are taken from two identical populations, one from each, the difference between them would be expected most probably to be a small one.

Two army units have different physical training programmes. One is more rigorous than the other and is presumed to impart better physical fitness. Unknown to us, Unit A personnel do have a higher fitness rate than Unit B. As we don't know this, the strategy would be to assume that there is no difference and test by sampling whether this hypothesis holds or not. Taking at-rest heart rates as a good indicator of fitness (the lower the better), randomly-selected training records of squaddies trained under both regimes are compared.

a)   The starting point in applying this theory is to assume that the two populations are identical, and that taking a sample from each of them is the same as taking two samples from one. The two samples means are from the sampling distribution of differences between means, introduced above, which looks like Figure 13.1.

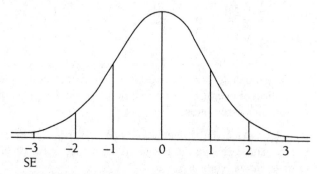

Fig. 13.1   Distribution of differences between sample means

The mean of differences = 0, since the sum of all the differences between pairs of means will equal 0. The distribution is normal, so 95% of the pairs would show a difference no greater than 1.96 standard errors (and 99% no more than 2.575 standard errors). This distribution asserts the hypothesis that $\mu_1 = \mu_2$.

b)   To test the assumption of similarity, we would state an alternative hypothesis, e.g. that $\mu_1 \neq \mu_2$, or that one is greater than the other.

c) An α-level would be set, to determine the critical value for the test.

d)   The difference between the sample means will be measured by subtraction, and that difference expressed as the number of standard errors by which they are separated.

e) The difference will be deemed to be by chance if it lies within the critical value limits, and we will accept that the populations are alike. The difference will be regarded as statistically significant if it exceeds the critical value; we would accept at the chosen α-level of confidence that the two populations are not alike.

f) α is the measure of risk that, in deciding the two populations are not the same, we would be making the wrong decision.

Figure 13.2 illustrates the difference between Unit A personnel and Unit B personnel.

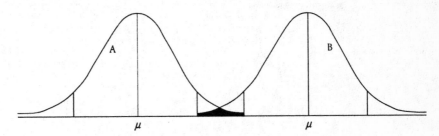

Fig. 13.2   Sampling distribution of means of two populations

The two curves are the sampling distributions of the means of the two populations, with their 95% error areas. The problem area is the shaded area where the two curves overlap. Common sense tells us that the two curves will overlap.

a) Members of both groups could exhibit a range of heart-rate values, so that some of B *could* be lower than some of A, and vice versa. If the two groups were so different that this is incredible, it would never have been supposed in the first place that they *might* have been similar.

b) The sampling distributions are in theory open-ended. Even if the two curves were drawn some distance apart, in theory the curves could overlap.

In rejecting the hypothesis of similarity because the difference passed into the shaded area, we are therefore 95% probably correct, but 5% possibly wrong. This is the sort of confidence we can enjoy even when we do not know the answer beforehand.

So much for theory – now we'll try a concrete example.

Procedure

A study was made of the number of days of sick leave per year taken by librarians and secondary school teachers. 65 librarians took an average of 9.6 days, with a standard deviation of 1.9. 55 teachers averaged 8.4 days, with a standard deviation of 2.3. At the α–level of 0.01, is the difference between the two groups statistically significant?

1   State the null hypothesis: $H_0 : \mu_1 = \mu_2$.
2   Choose an alternative hypothesis. In this case, perhaps, take the view that teachers take less time off than librarians, so $H_1 : \mu_1 < \mu_2$ regarding teachers as population 1 and librarians as population 2.
3   State the α–level (given here as 0.01).
4   Determine the critical value of z – as this is a one-tailed test at 0.01 the critical value must be -2.33z. (Minus, because we want to show that one group is 'less than' the other). See Figure 13.3.

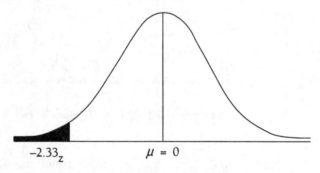

-2.33_z $\qquad\qquad\qquad \mu = 0$

Fig. 13.3   A test for the difference between two means

5   Subtract the sample means, and divide the difference by the standard error of the sampling distribution of differences from which these two means have been taken. The standard error of the distribution is estimated from the statistics of the two samples, by the formula:

$$\sigma\,(\bar{x}_1 - \bar{x}_2) = \sqrt{\frac{s_1^2}{n_1} + \frac{s_2^2}{n_1}}$$

where s_1 and s_2 equals sample 1 and sample 2, and the difference is calculated as:

$$z = \frac{\bar{x}_1 - \bar{x}_2}{\sqrt{\dfrac{s_1^2}{n_1} + \dfrac{s_2^2}{n_2}}}$$

In this example:

$$z = \frac{8.4 - 9.6}{\sqrt{2.3^2 + 1.9^2}} = \frac{1.2}{0.3895} = 3.0808$$

As −3.08 is beyond our critical value of −2.33, the limit of difference we can attribute to chance, the difference is deemed to be statistically significant at the 99% level of confidence. On the whole, teachers do take less time off than librarians.

Questions

1 In an experimental study of the provision of a public online service, the average time spent online searching requests direct from the public was 20.1 minutes, with a standard deviation of 3.6 minutes, based on a random sample of 52 searches. The equivalent data for 'inhouse' searches were 18.3, 2.8 and 33.

Is there a significant difference (with α at 0.05) in the time spent online for the different search types? What would be the effect on your conclusions if α were set at 0.01?

2 Because of financial cutbacks, a library committee instructs the librarian to close one of two branches which are in the same district. In making the choice, the librarian takes into account the relative amount of use made of each branch. Part of his evidence is the average daily issue of each, based on samples. He samples 52 days at Branch X and finds a mean of 2315 loans, with $s = 741$; at Branch Z he samples 49 days and finds a mean of 2622 with $s = 913$. Can the librarian conclude, at $\alpha = 0.05$, that the true mean daily issue is higher at Branch Z?

3 A new procedure for dealing with interlibrary loans is considered for introduction into a library. Staff are divided into two groups, one using the present method, and the other, after suitable training, testing the new method.

Group A (new method) processes 150 requests in a mean time of 5.5 minutes, with a standard deviation of 1.7 minutes.

Group B (old method) processes 100 requests in a mean time of 6 minutes, with a standard deviation of 2 minutes. Is the new method faster?

Test for the significance of the difference between mean times, with $\alpha = 0.05$, and interpret the result.

Chapter 14
Proportions

Summary

Proportions can be dealt with by the same operations that we
have learned to do with means. Here you see how the logic of
inference already learned can apply to this different type of
statistic.

A proportion is simply a subset of a larger group. It is expressed symbolically as

$$\frac{x}{n} \text{ i.e. } \frac{\text{how often has the characteristic been counted}}{\text{in a given number of trials?}}$$

A high level of measurement is not necessary. The lowest level, the 'categorical', or
'nominal', level can be used. This kind of data is called 'count data' – it is enough
that an individual possesses or exhibits the characteristic in which you are interested.
How much of the characteristic is shown, or how often, it is not necessary to
measure.

A reader comes to the library on half-day closing, or does not. Stock-taking
shows that an item is missing, or it is not. What proportion of items on loan are
borrowed by users from a particular part of town? What proportion of regular users
are male?

The results of enquiries of like these are of the simple Yes–No type. We can see,
then, that proportions are *binomially distributed*, not normally-distributed.

In the population as a whole there will be a true proportion (i.e. a mean proportion) of the characteristic. Samples will show different proportions, of course, so
there will be a *sampling distribution of proportions*. This distribution will have its
'mean' proportion, i.e. the true proportion, symbolized as Π (some texts use p).

The standard deviation of this distribution is

$$\sigma = \frac{\sqrt{p.q}}{n}$$

As the details of the population are not usually known, the standard error has to be approximated from sample data.

You will remember that binomial distributions can be normal or skewed, depending on the size of p (probability of a success) and of q (i.e. $1 - p$). The distribution of proportions may, however, be regarded as approximately normal in shape under certain circumstances. When a sample is taken, and the proportion of the characteristic present is calculated, if the sample size is big enough for $n \times p$ to equal 5 or greater and for $n \times (1 - p)$ to equal 5 or greater, where p is the proportion observed in the sample and n is the size of the sample then the sample can be deemed to have come from a sampling distribution of proportions which is approximately normal.

Example: 11 students out of 70 asked said that they had part-time jobs. $11 \div 70 = 0.157$.

Does $n \times p = 5$ or greater? $0.157 \times 70 = 11$
Does $n (1 - p) = 5$ or greater? $0.843 \times 70 = 59$

So we can say that 0.157 is one proportion from a sampling distribution which is approximately normal.

Being able to assume normality puts us on familiar ground, as proportions can be tested against the Standard Normal Distribution.

The population has an overall true proportion, around which are distributed all the possible (large) sample proportions. As the distribution is normal, it is safe to say that 95% and 99% of them lie within the usual z-values of $1.96z$ and $2.575z$ respectively. This, then is the basis for calculating confidence intervals for a sample proportion, for testing a hypothesis for one sample proportion, and for testing the difference between proportions of two samples.

When the sample proportion is near to 0.5, the approximation to a normal distribution is closest. If p is nearer to 0 or to 1, the approximation can't be so easily assumed – the sample has to be large enough to pass the test shown above.

Confidence intervals for population Π

Where proportions are normally-distributed, the standard error of the sampling distribution of proportions is:

$$\sqrt{\frac{p_s (1 - p_s)}{n}}$$

A confidence interval is calculated from the formula:

$$CI = p_s \pm (z \frac{\alpha}{2} \times \sqrt{\frac{p_s(1 - p_s)}{n}})$$

121

so for the example of students with part-time jobs:

$$95\% \text{ CI } = 0.157 \pm (1.96 \times \sqrt{\frac{0.157 \times 0.843}{70}})$$

which = 0.157 ± 0.0852, giving a confidence interval of

$$0.0718 < \Pi < 0.242$$

Another example:
If 400 people are a random sample of shoppers who try a new brand of coffee, and 136 say they like it and will buy it regularly, make a 95% confidence interval for the true proportion who will buy this coffee.

$$p_s = \frac{136}{400} = 0.34$$

Test for normality: in this case $n \times p$ and $n \times (1 - p)$ are well above 5.

$$95\% \text{ CI } = 0.34 \pm (1.96 \times \sqrt{\frac{0.34 \times 0.66}{400}})$$

$$= 0.34 \pm 0.046$$
$$= 0.294 < \Pi < 0.386$$

Hypothesis testing of a proportion

We start with a belief in a figure as the true proportion of a phenomenon in a population. This proportion is tested as the hypothetical proportion p_0. For example, a railways regional controller boasts that no more than 4% of his trains arrive late at their destinations. Sceptical of this claim, a passengers' watchdog group observe a random selection of services across the region over a period of time and find that 23 out of 430 services arrived late. This sample proportion p_s is 0.053.

Is the difference between p_0 (0.04) and p_s (0.053) due only to sampling variation, or does it indicate that the official figure is an underestimate?

We first assume a population (of train services in the region) whose mean proportion of late trains is 0.04. Because of the size of the sample, we can say that the sampling distribution of proportions approximates to a normal distribution. Any sample from this population, therefore, is subject to the usual probabilities of being from the central 95% or 99% or outside them. The difference between p_0 and p_s will be calculated as a number of standard errors and compared to a critical value.

State the null hypothesis: $H_0 : \Pi = 0.04$
Choose an alternative hypothesis. In this case it would be reasonable to choose
$H_1 : \Pi > 0.04$
$\alpha = 0.05$, $CV_z = 1.645$
$p_0 = 0.04$, $p_s = 0.053$

If a sample had shown a proportion less than 0.04, the matter could have been dropped, as it would seem to support the controller's claim. As the sample proportion is greater then 0.04, the question is, is it *significantly* more? Within the CV, the difference can be attributed to chance. Beyond it, the null hypothesis will be rejected, and the difference declared to be statistically significant.

The standard error of the sampling distribution is given its best estimate by assuming that the hypothesized proportion is correct, and using the formula:

$$\sqrt{\frac{p_0(1-p_0)}{n}}$$

The test statistic for the sample is therefore:

$$z = \frac{p_s - p_0}{\sqrt{\frac{p_0(1-p_0)}{n}}}$$

$$= \frac{0.053 - 0.04}{\sqrt{\frac{0.04 \times 0.96}{430}}} = \frac{0.013}{0.00945} = 1.376$$

The test shows a difference of less than the critical value. It is within the 95% of variation that can be attributed to chance, so the difference is not statistically significant and the controller's claim is upheld.

Testing the difference between two proportions

The logic and procedure are the same as that for a test between two sample means.

We start with the proposition that two populations exhibit the characteristic in the same measure. If we asked the entire student populations of two similar-sized colleges, 'Do you read *The Guardian*?' we should expect to find the same proportion in each answering 'Yes'. Supposing, of course, that one college didn't have a pronounced leaning to the Left! If we took a *sample* from each college, we would expect to find them showing different proportions of Guardian readers, but the difference would not be significant.

If our proposition is true, then each population will have an identical sampling distribution of proportions. Taking each sample proportion of one population from each sample proportion of the other would result in a *sampling distribution of differences between proportions*, which would be approximately normal, and whose mean difference would be zero.

Two samples are taken to test the proposition that equal numbers in each college read *The Guardian*.

College 1 readers:

$$\frac{x_1}{n_1} = \frac{44}{175} = 0.25 = p_{s_1}$$

College 2 readers:

$$\frac{x_2}{n_2} = \frac{34}{125} = 0.27 = p_{s_2}$$

p_{s_1} = the proportion of sample 1
p_{s_2} = the proportion of sample 2

The difference between the two proportions (0.25 - 0.27 = −0.02) belongs to the theoretical sampling distribution of differences between proportions (which we are assuming exists if our proposition is true). Is the difference due only to sampling variation, or is it significant?

The null hypothesis is always that the true proportions of the two populations are the same:

$$H_0 : \Pi_1 = \Pi_2$$

The alternative hypotheses are as before:

e.g. for this question: $H_1 : \Pi_1 = \Pi_2$

This question is tested at $\alpha = 0.05$, $\therefore$ CV$_z = 1.96$.

The difference between p_{s_1} and p_{s_2} has to be divided by the standard error of the sampling distribution, which is estimated from the data of the two samples. The formula for the standard error is:

$$\sqrt{\frac{p_p(1-p_p)}{n_1} + \frac{p_p(1-p_p)}{n_2}}$$

where p_p is the *pooled proportion*. The pooled proportion is calculated from:

$$\frac{x_1 + x_2}{n_1 + n_2} \quad \text{and never from:} \quad \frac{x_1}{n_1} + \frac{x_2}{n_2}$$

i.e. in this case:

$$\frac{44 + 34}{175 + 125} = 0.26 \quad \text{and not} \quad \frac{44}{175} + \frac{34}{125} = 0.52$$

The formula for the test is therefore:

$$z = \frac{p_{s_1} - p_{s_2}}{\sqrt{\frac{p_p(1-p_p)}{n_1} + \frac{p_p(1-p_p)}{n_2}}}$$

for the example:

$$z = \frac{0.25 - 0.27}{\sqrt{\dfrac{0.26 \times 0.74}{175} + \dfrac{0.26 \times 0.74}{125}}} = -0.389$$

The calculated difference between the two sample proportions is less than the difference that can be attributed to sampling chance, i.e. less than the critical value of z, so the null hypothesis is accepted. The difference is not thought to be statistically significant at the chosen level of significance.

Questions

1 A library authority considers opening one of its libraries on Wednesday afternoons (when it is closed at present) and will do so if it can be shown that 75% of library users want this change. The opinions of a sample of 120 are canvassed, and the sample shows that 83 express themselves in favour. At the 99% level of confidence ($\alpha = 0.01$) does this sample support the idea that 75% of the users do in fact want the extra opening?

2 In a study of 'reader failure at the shelf', the hypothesis was tested that 35% of failures were due to incorrect catalogue use. A random sample of 400 'failures' were investigated and it was found that 128 were due to incorrect catalogue use. At $\alpha = 0.01$, do the data support the hypothesis?

3 Do two branch libraries' users make similar use of the book reservations facility? Random samples of readers were asked if they had made any reservations during the last six months. In library A, 19 out of 50 said Yes, and in library B 12 out of 40 said Yes. Is the difference significant at $\alpha = 0.05$?

4 In random sample of microcomputers produced at two different plants, 16 out of 200 machines at plant A were found to need servicing before despatch, and 20 out of 400 at plant B. At the 0.05 level of significance would you have anything to say to the quality control managers at the plants?

Chapter 15
Bivariate statistics

Summary

This chapter and the next deal with questions about possible relationships between two variables in a population. Their dependence or independence are tested by two groups of measures. Tests for association study the co-occurrence of events, and are measured at the nominal levels of measurement. Variables on the interval/ratio scales are tested for correlation, the extent to which changes in one variable reflect changes in the other. The tests of χ^2, Pearson's correlation and Spearman's correlation are particularly noted.

Association of two variables

So far we have been drawing inferences from one variable (univariate statistics). A researcher may be interested in bivariate statistics, i.e. those examining the relationship between two variables. Do reading lists, for instance, encourage students to use the library more than if they were not given reading lists? Is there more stress among male than female staff due to library budget cuts?

Probability, as we have seen, is concerned with events, whether they happen or not, and how strong is the likelihood that they will happen or not. The question may now be asked, whether two events show an overall tendency to happen *together*. In other words, is there an 'association' between them?

A 'tendency' to occur together means that it will not necessarily happen every time, at each 'trial', but that in the population that is being sampled this tendency exists overall.

A related and important question is, *how strong* is that association? Is it statistically significant, and is it significant in the sense that the researcher need take any notice of it, or base any decisions or actions upon the result? Many samples will in fact produce a coefficient of association, but it may not necessarily be significant in the action/decision sense.

Data may be recorded on nominal, ordinal, or interval/ratio scales, and different tests are appropriate to each.

With these preliminary thoughts in mind, we'll look into the notion of association with examples at the nominal level ('count data') and with variables that are dichotomous, i.e. having only two values.

Since two events will either occur, or not occur, and they may or may not happen together, we could view the possible outcomes in a simple table:

	Y	Not Y
X	a	b
Not X	c	d

This is called a contingency table. It shows the possible relationships of events

The letters in the four cells represent the probabilities (or frequencies) of the possible outcomes.

a	is the event that both X and Y will occur
d	is the event that neither X nor Y will occur
b	is the event that X will occur, but not Y
c	is the event that Y will occur, but not X

Think about this matrix for a few moments. It will be obvious that the larger the figure in cell a (compared to b, c, and d) the stronger will be the association between X and Y. The other cells recognize that sometimes X and Y will *not* occur together.

Think about the opposite case. If the figures in a and c are the same, and those in b and d are the same, then it doesn't matter whether the members of the sample are X or *Not X* – their responses to the second variable Y will be the same, i.e. there is no association that makes Y tend to occur when X occurs.

In fact, tests of association are based on the assumption that there is *no* association. It then falls to the researcher to demonstrate that such an association exists.

Yule's Q

To bring all this theory down to earth, we'll take an everyday example – whether in a population men are more likely to smoke than are women. A sample produced the following scores:

	Y (Smokers)	Not Y (Non-smokers)
X (Men)	a 52	b 28
Not X (Women)	c 50	d 70

On the face of it, the relationship between men and smoking (0.65 of the men in the sample) is greater than the relationship between women and smoking (only 0.416). The relationship may be more apparent than real, since the groups of men and women are so different in size, so a test is needed. We know that another sample may show the opposite picture, but if the association of men and smoking is generally greater in the population, another sample would *probably* confirm it.

Yule's coefficient of association, or *Yule's Q*, compares the cells *a*, *b*, *c* and *d* in the formula:

$$Q = \frac{ad - bc}{ad + bc}$$

Taking figures from our sample:

$$\frac{(52 \times 70) - (28 \times 50)}{(52 \times 70) + (28 \times 50)} = \frac{3640 - 1400}{3640 + 1400} = 0.4 \text{ rec.}$$

There is a *positive* association between *X* (men) and *Y* (smoking), i.e. the more variable *X* occurs, the more likely is variable *Y* to occur with it. If *a* × *d* is greater than *b* × *c*, an association will be positive.

If the sample figures had been reversed, they would have suggested that more women smoked than men, i.e. $\frac{28 \mid 52}{70 \mid 50} = \frac{1400 - 3640}{1400 + 3640} = -0.4 \text{ rec.}$

This would be called *negative* association, i.e. the more *X* (men) the less *Y* (smoking). This will happen when *a* × *d* is less than *b* × *c* .

Suppose now that the true situation in a population is that men and women in equal proportions smoke. If the sample reflected this, the scores *might* look like:

	Smoke	Don't
Men	52	28
Women	52	28

Yule's *Q* calculates as zero.

Since *a* × *d* = *b* × *c*, there is no association between gender and smoking, i.e. no *difference* between men and women in this respect.

Interpretation

In practice, a symmetrical result like the contrived one shown in the preceding paragraph is unlikely, though a sample which approximates the true state of affairs in more likely than one which does not. The problem is that a set of figures *will* produce a coefficient of association, in most cases. If we doctor the symmetrical figures to show a slight inequality, (slightly more men than women – hardly enough to support a case, given the randomness of sampling):

54	26
52	28

Q calculates as 0.056

There is undeniably a positive association, but it is very small, compared with the 0.4 we got earlier. How would it compare with a coefficient of, say, 0.9, which is an almost perfect association (nearly all men, but hardly any women, smoke)? There is no firm rule about this and each researcher would have an individual valuation.

The value of Yule's Q

Q gives a digestible explanation of the theory of association. It is a simple test to use, and available for simple (nominal) data. Besides showing the presence of an association, it gives a measure of the strength of that association. It does not, however, affirm the *statistical significance* of the association, so the association could be due only to sampling variation.

Chi-square (χ^2)

Yule's Q can only be applied to 2×2 association tests. Often it is desired to test for association where variables take on more than two values. For this the χ^2 test is useful. This test can be used on data collected on a *nominal* scale. Its weakness is that while it shows the statistical significance of an association it does not show its strength.

Readers in three branch libraries, in different areas of a town, are asked whether they would be willing to pay a small charge for borrowing videos. The libraries are sited in different types of area – one middle-class residential, one mixed residential, one with a preponderance of retired people. The argument is that users from each area would be willing in equal proportions to pay a charge, i.e. that there is no association between area and level of response. The χ^2 test assumes that there is no association, that the two variables of place and willingness are independent.

The figures recorded are as follows:

	Library 1	Library 2	Library 3	
Willing	82	66	123	271
Not willing	36	32	75	143
	118	98	198	414

The figures in the six 'cells' within the lines are the *observed frequencies*. They are simply the responses that have been counted into the appropriate boxes.

At first glance there are noticeable differences amongst the 'willing' responses (82, 66, 123). These differences are less apparent when we reflect that the figures are related to the differing sizes of the samples from which they come (118, 98,198). The 'willing' figures are *proportions* of the totals asked the question at each library. $82/118 = 0.695$; $66/98 = 0.673$; $123/198 = 0.62$.

The differences between the proportions are not so great as the bare figures at first suggested. Are the differences merely due to chance, or do they amount to a statistically significant difference in attitudes? In other words, are more users at Library 1 willing to pay than at Library 3?

Null hypothesis. As stated, the assumption behind a χ^2 test is that there is no association, that the two variables are *independent*, that the true proportions are the same in the three populations:

i.e. $H_0 : \Pi_1 = \Pi_2 = \Pi_3$

The χ^2 test

1   The test involves calculating what the proportions *would have been* if the null hypothesis were true.

2   It then calculates how far each *observed* figure deviates from what would have been *expected*, and the deviations are rendered into a single figure, the sample χ^2.

3   This figure is tested against a sampling distribution to determine its significance.

Out of the 414 people responding, 271 were 'willing'. This is a proportion of 0.654589. It means that the proportion of 'not willing' responses is 0.345411, which is $1 - 0.654589$. (It is not usual to express proportions to 5 or 6 decimal places, but we'll stay with these figures for the moment). If the variables are independent, we would expect the libraries to return the same proportion of 'willing' responses. Library 1's 118 responses would therefore have shown $118 \times 0.654589 = 77.24$ as willing to pay. Similarly, the proportions of 98 and 198 would be 64.15 and 129.61. (Don't be disturbed by the idea of fractions of people!)

The 'not willing' figures must be adjusted also, by multiplying them by 0.345411.

Our table now shows the original *observed* frequencies and the hypothetical *expected* figures.

	Library 1	Library 2	Library 3	
Willing	82	66	123	271
	77.24	64.15	129.61	
Not willing	36	32	75	143
	40.76	33.85	68.39	
	118	98	198	414

Check that the expected figures add up to the row and column totals. There is something wrong if they do not.

Fortunately, there is a simpler way to arrive at the expected figures. All the observed figures in the cells, and row and column totals, are proportions of the total 414 respondents. On the assumption that all the libraries are equal in their readers' attitudes to the question, we can multiply the proportion 'willing' by the proportion 'Library 1', and express that as a fraction of the total respondents, repeating this for the other libraries. In other words, we address each cell in turn, multiply *its* row total by *its* column total, dividing the product by the overall total, or:

$$\frac{r \times c}{N}$$

So, for example, $271 \times 118 \div 414 = 77.24$. Try this for the other cells, to verify that the expected figures are the same as already found.

Deviations of the expected values from the observed values

These deviations may be due only to chance in the sample. Applying the argument earlier in this chapter (see Yule's Q calculated as zero), if the proportions were equal then each O figure would be the same as its E figure. A *sample* would show some deviations, and we have the by-now-familiar argument that a small difference from $\Pi 1 = \Pi 2 = \Pi 3$ would not make us change our mind, but a large difference might. How large a difference would be needed?

Besides the null hypothesis, we need to specify a level of alpha and find the appropriate critical value from the χ^2 table. (See the section on critical values later in this chapter). For this example, $\alpha = 0.05$, degrees of freedom (df) = 2, giving a critical value of 5.991.

χ^2 for the sample, which is the value of the total deviations of E from O, is calculated by the formula:

$$\chi^2 = \Sigma \frac{(O - E)^2}{E}$$

Take each cell in turn (the order is not important) and deal with the pairs of figures as follows: the difference between each E and O figure is squared, to remove signs, and the squared figure is divided by the expected one. The total of the final column is the χ^2 for the sample:

O	E	$O - E$	$(O - E)^2$	$(O - E)^2/E$
82	77.24	4.76	22.6576	0.2933402
66	64.15	1.85	3.4225	0.0533515
123	129.61	−6.61	43.6921	0.3371043
36	40.76	−4.76	22.6576	0.5558783
32	33.85	−1.85	3.4225	0.1011078
75	68.39	6.61	43.6921	0.6388667

$$\chi^2 = 1.9796488$$

Conclusion

The critical value of 5.991 is the largest calculated χ^2 that would allow us to retain the null hypothesis of independence. Since the calculated figure is well within this limit, we conclude that there is no difference in the level of 'willing' responses from the three libraries, i.e. that there is no association between place and response.

Critical values of χ^2

Use of the χ^2 table involves the concept of *degrees of freedom* (df). In any row of cells, all the figures but one are 'free' to take on any value. The remaining cell must have the value that makes up the total of the values in the row. The same applies to *columns* of cells. It doesn't particularly matter which cells, but to determine the degrees of freedom active in a sample we discount one row of cells and one column of cells and count the remaining cells.

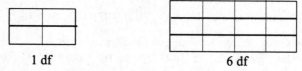

1 df   6 df

The discounted cells must, of course, be included in the calculation of sample χ^2 as shown above.

The table we use (see Appendix 2) is a partial table, with columns headed $\chi^2.05$ and $\chi^2.01$, for the two usual levels of α. Read down the df column to the correct degree of freedom, and select the critical value from the appropriate column.

The distribution of χ^2 has a different curve for each degree of freedom, but Figure 15.1 shows it distributed from zero association:

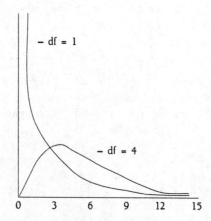

Fig. 15.1   Distribution of χ^2 from zero association

The larger the calculated sample χ^2, the greater the chance that it is significant, though significance is determined according to where the critical value is placed on the horizontal scale.

Goodness-of-fit tests

The χ^2 test can be used in cases where there is a known pattern of a phenomenon in a population.

Suppose five machines producing a particularly fine component are known from experience consistently to produce 5% faulty components, on average. How could the quality control manager discover if one or more machines had deteriorated in performance?

A random sample of 100 components in one day's output from each machine might yield the following numbers of faulty components:

8   2   7   11   4

Since the machines were expected to produce only 5 faulty units in every 100, is the variation due only to sampling chance, or to something worse? We have the expected figures and the observed figures, so we can apply the χ^2 test, taking α as 0.01.

Observed	8	2	7	11	4
Expected	5	5	5	5	5

df = 4 (discount 1 column, no row to discount). $CV\chi^2 = 13.277$

Calculate χ^2 as before; it calculates to 11.8. As this is within the critical value, the limit of belief in the null hypothesis, we conclude that, while machine no. 4 might bear watching, overall the machines are behaving normally.

Where there is no accepted standard of performance, expected figures can be derived by averaging the observed ones. Example: Interlibrary loan requests might be related to the days of the week. A random sample from records shows that average requests over a period were as follows.

M	T	W	Th	F	
27	23	18	13	39	total 120

Divide the 120 equally, on the assumption that all days are equal, and that differences are due only to chance.

	M	T	W	Th	F	
O	27	23	18	13	39	total 120
E	24	24	24	24	24	

Testing this at $\alpha = 0.05$, df = 4, $CV\chi^2 = 9.488$.

Sample χ^2 calculates at 16.3, which is beyond the critical value. We can conclude then that requests are influenced by the day of the week, and the observed figures give the clue to which days are busiest.

Questions

1 Three course leaders complained to each other about student absences from lectures. They compiled figures from a sample of days picked from the registers and presented the following:

	Absent	Not absent
Course 1	26	68
Course 2	65	120
Course 3	77	215

   a) For each course, express the Absent figure as a simple proportion of the students on that course.
   b) Conduct a χ^2 test, with $\alpha = 0.05$, to determine whether the apparent differences in the proportions have arisen by chance or are statistically significant.

2 Students in a college are randomly selected to be given a test in using the library catalogues. The test measures success in finding certain items, and results are listed by students' faculties.

Success	Engng	FACULTY Science	Social Science	Art
Always	18	29	70	115
Sometimes	17	28	30	41
Never	11	10	11	20

   At the level of significance of 0.01, test whether there is any relationship between a student's faculty and success in using the catalogues.

3 A senior librarian in a large system observes that staff absences seem to be related to the day of the week. She collects the following data from over a year:

	Mon	Tue	Wed	Thu	Fri
Total absences for the year	302	285	255	267	298

   Carry out a goodness-of-fit test which assumes an equal distribution of absences to see whether there is a relationship between absences and days of the week. $\alpha = 0.05$.

Chapter 16
Correlation and regression

Summary

This final chapter examines how the relationship between variables is identified and measured by correlation tests and how patterns of relationship may be sought in models of regression.

What are correlation and regression?

Logically, regression precedes correlation, as the second is a step towards the first.

Regression is concerned with prediction. Do two variables have an association in a population, an association strong enough to allow us to take a value of one variable and predict the corresponding value of the other? For example, could a manufacturer relate values of sales to the amount spent on advertising? Are issues related to sizes of lending stocks? Is there a generally-true relationship between numbers of library staff and population served?

As with the notion of association, it may not be wise to conclude a cause-and-effect relationship necessarily. Regression and correlation attempt to assess the covariance of two variables. As people grow taller, do they also become heavier? If unemployment rises, do sales of luxuries correspondingly decrease? Would it be possible to relate a given height to an expected weight?

While there may be a general correspondence of two variables, it may not always be a perfect one-to-one correspondence. If for every 1000 more unemployed reported crime rose by 5%, a scatter diagram would look like Figure 16.1. Each dot represents scores on the two variables for one place. There will no doubt be other factors beside unemployment which affect crime figures, e.g. drug dependence, socioeconomic characteristics of an area, and others, so points may lie close to the line but not all on it.

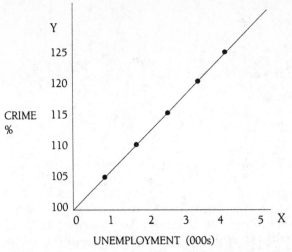

Fig. 16.1   Scatter diagram showing unemployment and crime correlation

Assumptions

1   For each value of the X variable, Y-scores can take on a range of values, because more than one factor affects the degree of presence of the Y variable.

2   It must be possible to assume that we can ignore these 'disturbance' factors, because they are unimportant and are unrelated to each other. If we can't make these assumptions, multiple regression, which is outside the scope of this text, will be necessary.

3   *Assumption of normality.* Unless there are compelling reasons against the belief (and often we can't really know), it is to be assumed that both X and Y variables are normally distributed. Both X and Y must be assumed to be *stochastic* variables, that is that they behave randomly, and the investigator has no control over what values are recorded – these are due only to chance.

For every value of X, Y can take on any value from a range that is normally-distributed. Similarly, for every value of Y, X can take on a range of values. This relationship is difficult to show in a diagram, so look at the Y values only in Figure 16.2.

From what we know of the properties of normal distributions, it can be expected that central values will be more likely to occur than peripheral ones. If the two variables are indeed closely related in the population, the distribution of Y for each value of X will have a very small standard deviation. If the close relation is true of Y to X, it will necessarily be true of X to Y, and the points plotted will deviate only slightly from a straight line relationship. If the relationship is weak, the standard deviation will be bigger, and observations will deviate more widely.

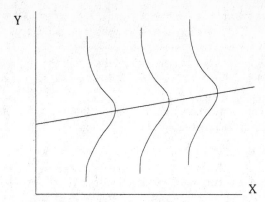

Fig. 16.2   Variability of *Y* against value of *X*

The sloping line on the graphs is called the regression line, or the 'line of best fit'. When its position is accurately calculated, values of *Y* can be read off against the line for any value of *X*. The line can be drawn on a diagram wherever the investigator thinks it fits best, but in this case it remains at best a subjective opinion.

Correlation measures the spread of observations about the regression line. It shows what kind of relationship exists, and how strong or weak that relationship is.

A scatter diagram like that on unemployment and crime is a useful starting point. Each plotted dot is in fact two measurements, showing the convergence of unemployment and crime for a given locality. If the dots are on a straight line, or very close, we could say that the diagram indicates a *strong positive correlation*. As *X* rises, so does *Y*. If the dots are more scattered, as in Figure 16.3, the correlation is still positive, but weaker. The more scattered they are, the weaker, and possibly non-existent, is the correlation.

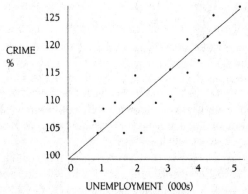

Fig. 16.3   Correlation between unemployment and crime figures

Negative correlation exists when Y decreases as X rises. As more people hire videos for home viewing, cinema attendances might decrease. Negative correlation can also range from strong to weak.

Zero correlation means there is so much scatter of observations that no pattern is clearly visible. The relationship, if it exists at all, is too weak to be of any great value in prediction by regression.

The value of a scatter diagram is that it gives a quick indication of whether it is worthwhile proceeding to a correlation test.

Tests for correlation

There are two major measures of correlation. Karl Pearson's 'product-moment coefficient of correlation' method is used when assumption of normality in the variables is possible. It is used when variables have been measured on an interval or ratio scale.

Spearman's rank-order correlation is employed when the variables are measured on an ordinal scale. Spearman's test is also useful when we cannot assume normality in the variables.

Pearson's r

Heights and weights of a random selection of 10 first-year college students are observed as follows:

		Height (in)	Weight (lb)
Student	A	64	144
	B	70	190
	C	66	141
	D	67	127
	E	69	166
	F	61	116
	G	67	180
	H	72	201
	I	66	160
	J	68	173

The scatter diagram for these data shows an overall positive correlation. The 'line of best fit' doesn't give a *measure* of the closeness between the independent variable (height) and the dependent variable (weight), so it can only be used with caution to relate height to weight.

Null hypothesis

The null hypothesis in all such tests is that there is no correlation, i.e. that $r = 0$. The alternative hypothesis is, of course, that a correlation does exist. If there is a correlation, it could be positive or negative, so these tests are always *two-tailed* tests.

$$-1 \text{--------} \boxed{\text{----- } 0 \text{ -----}} \text{--------}+1$$

The box in the centre represents the area alpha (α), that is, the probability that if the correlation is deemed to be significant and the null hypothesis is rejected, the decision would be wrong. The critical values that set the limits of α for any sample are taken from a table of critical values of r (not included in this text). A sample must show a coefficient of correlation greater than the critical value in order for it to be deemed statistically significant.

The test statistic

Pearson's r for a sample is calculated from the formula

$$r = \frac{\Sigma(x - \bar{x})(y - \bar{y})}{\sqrt{\Sigma(x - \bar{x})^2 \times \Sigma(y - \bar{y})^2}}$$

Each case, represented by two values, must be dealt with in turn under the following headings:

	x (heights)	$(x - \bar{x})$	y (weights)	$(y - \bar{y})$	$(x - \bar{x})^2$	$(y - \bar{y})^2$	$(x - \bar{x})(y - \bar{y})$
A	64	−3	144	−15.8	9	249.64	47.4
B	70	3	190	30.2	9	912.04	90.6
C	66	−1	141	−18.8	1	353.44	18.8
D	67	0	127	−32.8	0	1075.84	0
E	69	2	166	6.2	4	38.44	12.4
F	61	−6	116	−43.8	36	1918.44	262.8
G	67	0	180	20.2	0	408.04	0
H	72	5	201	41.2	25	1697.44	206
I	66	−1	160	0.2	1	0.04	0.2
J	68	1	173	13.2	1	174.24	13.2
					86	6827.6	651.4

$$\bar{x} = 67 \qquad\qquad \bar{y} = 159.8$$

Substituting the three totals into the formula:

$$r = \frac{651.4}{\sqrt{86 \times 6827.6}} = 0.85$$

0.85 would be regarded as a strong positive correlation, showing a general tendency for weight to increase as height increases.

Significance of r

The coefficient just calculated may be strong, but is it statistically significant? How good is it as an estimate of the correlation in the population? This depends on two factors:

1   The size of the coefficient. The nearer it is to a perfect correlation of 1 the less likely it is to have arisen purely by the chance of the sample.
2   The size of the sample. The more pairs of figures are involved in the coefficient, the more likely it is that we would find a similar coefficient if we took another sample.

This second factor is reflected in the table of critical values for *r*. For a small sample, the critical value is high (0.957 for *n* = 3 when α = 0.05) and lower for a larger sample (0.444 for *n* = 20). The larger the sample, the less rigorous is the test for significance.

To return to heights and weights – the critical value for *r*, when α = 0.025, and *n* = 10, is 0.632. Our coefficient for heights and weights is greater than that, so the correlation is deemed to be significant.

$$-1 \text{ -------- } |\text{------} 0 \text{ ------}| \text{ --------} 0.85 \text{ ----} +1$$
$$\phantom{-1 \text{ -------- }} -0.632 +0.632$$

The null hypothesis of no correlation, limited by the critical value, must therefore be rejected.

Interpretation

When a correlation is shown to be significant, its value to the researcher remains a matter for the researcher's own judgement, and judgement will include consideration of the size of the sample, other possible causes of weight, what the researcher intends to do as a result of the finding.

It is accepted that the square of the coefficient shows how much of the variation in *Y* is explained by variation in *X*. Height will explain 0.7225, or 72.25% (i.e. 0.85^2) of increases in height. Because squares are used, the higher the coefficient the greater the influence: 0.8 is not twice as great as 0.4, when squared, as $0.4^2 = 0.16$, while $0.8^2 = 0.64$.

Spearman's rank-correlation coefficient (r_s): correlation of ordinal-level data

Sometimes data is not measured on an interval scale, by necessity or choice. Scores may be on a ranked scale, e.g.: never/very infrequently/infrequently/frequently/very frequently.

Other variables which cannot be quantified precisely are leadership potential, popularity. Another kind is the use of assessment marks to indicate students' positions in a class, rather than regarding them as accurate measures of differences. For variables which are not normally distributed, or whose distributions are unknown, Spearman's would be a suitable test.

Example

Is there a correlation between cigarette smoking and incidence of chest complaints? Numbers of cigarettes smoked are recorded in ranked classes:

None/very few/few/many/very many

Frequency of chest complaints is categorized as:

None/very infrequent/infrequent/frequent/very frequent.

Five people gave their responses as:

	Cigarettes	Chest complaints
A	Very many	Frequent
B	Few	Infrequent
C	Many	Very frequent
D	None	Infrequent
E	Very few	None

These responses must be given ranking numbers 1 to 5, whether low-to-high or high-to-low doesn't matter, as long as both are done the same way.

This becomes:

	X rank	Y rank	d (i.e. $x-y$)	d^2
A	5	4	1	1
B	3	2.5	0.5	0.25
C	4	5	−1	1
D	1	2.5	−1.5	2.25
E	2	1	1	1
				$\overline{5.5}$

Tied ranks

In the Y column, only 4 of the possible 5 categories are used. This doesn't matter. The responses are:

None	Infrequent	Infrequent	Frequent	Very frequent
1	2	3	4	5

We can't logically rank the two Infrequents as 2 *and* 3, since they are the same level of response. They therefore share the value of the ranks and are both called 2.5.

A series of scores arranged in rank order can have numbers repeated, e.g.:

scores	12	13	14	14	14	15	16	.....
ranks	1	2	3	4	5	6	7	.....

As the three scores of 14 are the same, they can't be given different ranks, so they all have the average rank. $3 + 4 + 5 = 12$, $12/3 = 4$, so the three 14s all have the rank 4. After the tied ranks, other ranks continue as before, so, 1 2 4 4 4 6 7 ...

Returning to the table above, Y ranks are subtracted from X ranks, giving the column d. To remove the signs, figures in d are squared, and the sum of d^2 obtained.

Spearman's coefficient of correlation is found by:

$$r_s = 1 - \frac{6 \times \Sigma d^2}{n(n^2 - 1)}$$

For the sample:

$$r_s = 1 - \frac{6 \times 5.5}{5 \times 24} = 0.725$$

This is a strong positive correlation, but its significance must be tested.

Significance testing of r_s (small samples)

As with Pearson's test, the null hypothesis is that there is no correlation. $r_s = 0$, and the values of X and Y in each pair are randomly paired by chance.

There is a sampling distribution of r_s which for large samples is approximately normal. (Some authorities say that for samples as little as $n = 10$ the distribution is approximately normal.) The t distribution is used to test small samples for significance.

The test statistic for a small sample is:

$$t = r_s \sqrt{\frac{n - 2}{1 - r_s^2}}$$

Setting α at 0.025, we have to deduct 2 degrees of freedom – one for each variable – so $CV_t = 3.182$.

For the sample:

$$t = 0.725 \sqrt{\frac{3}{1 - 0.5256}} = 1.823$$

This figure is less than the critical value, so we have to retain the null hypothesis, and conclude that the correlation coefficient arose by sampling chance and is not significant at the 95% level of confidence.

Large samples

Where a sample can be classed as large, and the distribution of r_s taken as normal, the z-distribution can be used to test significance. The formula for this is:

$$z = r_s \sqrt{n-1}$$

Is there a correlation between hours of revision time on an examination subject, and marks gained in that examination? 10 students were asked to log the approximate time given to revision, and their responses were later compared with their marks.

X (hours)	X rank	Y (marks)	Y rank	d	d^2
6	3	56	4	−1	1
7	4.5	44	2	2.5	6.25
10	7	79	8	−1	1
12	8	72	7	1	1
9	6	70	6	0	0
4	2	54	3	−1	1
17	10	94	10	0	0
14	9	85	9	0	0
1	1	33	1	0	0
7	4.5	65	5	−0.5	0.25
					10.5

$$r_s = 1 - \frac{6 \times 10.5}{10 \times 99} = 0.936$$

This is a very strong coefficient. If its significance is tested at $\alpha = 0.025$, $CV_z = 1.96$.

$$z = 0.936\sqrt{9} = 2.81$$

This is well beyond the limit of no correlation, so the null hypothesis is rejected. Generally, revision time pays off in higher marks.

Regression analysis

Regression, as seen earlier, assesses whether it is possible to predict a value of one variable (such as production line outputs) by knowing something about another variable (such as workers' scores in speed-of-assembly tests.) It is said that one hangman worked out a table showing the ideal amount of rope to use, given the victim's weight!

The term 'regression' derives from a study of parents' and children's heights. Tall parents tended to have shorter children, and vice versa. Children tended to 'regress towards the mean'. If the difference between above average and below-average parents' and children's heights is not large, there is a good straight-line-fit and prediction can be good.

The value of regression for prediction is related to the strength of the correlation existing between two variables. If correlation is weak, a wide range of values of the dependent variable *Y* is possible for any value of the independent variable *X*. See the following graph:

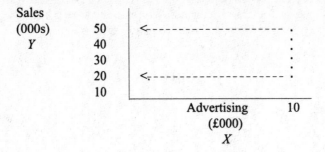

Such a wide range of scores observed against *X* = 10,000 would not be of much value to a sales director. A closer spread of scores would give a narrower range of possible outcomes on *Y*.

We saw that with correlation there is a difficulty about where to draw the line of best fit. For prediction, the line has to be drawn in the best possible position from the information in a sample.

Think through the following argument intuitively, referring back to the heights and weights example given earlier.

- Draw a line through the dots in what seems like a reasonable position.
- For each value of *X* there will be two values of *Y*:
  1) where the plotted dot actually is and
  2) where *X* strikes the line of best fit. These are called *Y* and *Y* prime (*Y′*).

This is shown for just two of the dots.

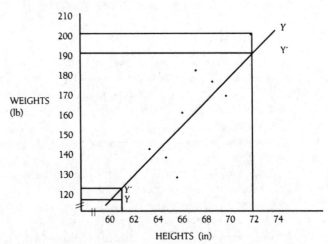

Fig. 16.4 Scatter diagram showing *Y* and *Y* prime

- Measure the difference between each Y and its companion Y'.
- Square the differences – to be rid of minus signs.
- Add the total of the squares.
- Move the line repeatedly and repeat the calculation until the total of squares is the smallest figure obtainable. Where the sum of squares is least is the correct position for the line.

Fortunately such a tedious process is unnecessary, but it makes the point that the line is correctly placed when it deviates least from all the plotted dots.

Simple linear regression involves the law of the straight line, i.e. $Y = a + b.x$, or more correctly Y', since we are interested in the 'correct' value of Y against a value of X, not what was observed in the sample.

a is the value of Y (+ or –) when $X = 0$, that is, where the line effectively begins
b is the average change in Y for each unit of X, i.e. the angle of rise of the line
X values are the ones which are known
Y' are the values we want to relate to those on X.

Calculating the position of the regression line uses what are called the *normal equations*. They are:

$$\Sigma y = na + b(\Sigma x)$$
$$\Sigma xy = a(\Sigma x) + b(\Sigma x^2)$$

For a collection of paired values (here 10) we need 4 totals:

Heights	Weights		
x	y	x^2	xy
64	152	4096	9728
70	200	4900	14000
66	148	4356	9768
....			
....			
etc.			
Σx 670	Σy 1684	Σx^2 44976	Σxy 113514

Using the simultaneous equations method we can discover the value of a and b from the sample. Substituting into the normal equations we have:

1. $1684 = 10a + 670b$
2. $113514 = 670a + 44976b$

Multiply 1. by 67 and 2. by 1 to equalize a in both lines.

1. $112828 = 670a + 44890b$
2. $113514 = 670a + 44976b$

Subtract line 1 from line 2, giving:

$$686 = 86b, \text{ so } b = \frac{686}{86} = 7.98 \text{ rounded}$$

Knowing b, it can be substituted into one of the original equations. Substituting into line 1:

$1684 = 10a + 670 \ (7.98)$
$1684 = 10a + 5346.6$
$1684 - 5346.6 = 10a$
$-366.26 = a$

The equation of the least squares line for the regression of Y on X for the sample is therefore

$y' = a + bx$,

or $y' = -366.26 + 7.98x$

To use this information to draw the regression line on a graph it is only necessary to calculate y' for a low value and a high value. Taking $x = 61, y' = -366.26 + 7.98(61)$ $= 120.52\text{lb}$.

Similarly, taking $x = 72, y' = -366.26 + 7.98(72) = 208.3\text{lb}$.

120.52 and 208.3 can be plotted as closely as practicable on a graph, and a line drawn between them.

One would be cautious about extrapolating beyond the range of x in the sample, but given that the correlation coefficient for these figures was 0.856 – a strong correlation – predicting expected heights for values of x within the range would give a reasonably close estimate.

Questions

1   The Pearson test.

Is there a correlation between the number of nursing staff in hospitals and the number of support staff (clerical, etc.) that are employed? Figures were obtained from 10 hospitals.

X (nursing)	Y (clerical)	
63	62	
38	30	
52	41	
58	31	$\alpha = 0.025$ (i.e. 0.05)
88	48	$CV_r = 0.632$.
85	42	
37	20	

62	38
93	50
44	28

2 The Spearman test.

Public libraries commonly use issue statistics as output measures. If issues could be shown to correlate positively with, for example, numbers of reference questions satisfied, this would strengthen confidence in the use of issue statistics as a general measure for evaluating libraries. The figures below show annual issues and numbers of queries satisfied in a random sample of 12 public library service points.

Calculate the Spearman coefficient and test the significance of the coefficient if $\alpha = 0.01$.

x issues (000s)	y queries (00s)
41	43
37.5	36
50.5	48
46	44
35.5	31
40.3	42
42.1	38
27.9	30
18.6	21
33.7	36
53.4	51
30.7	24

3 From published statistics it is possible to sample libraries and note the books on loan at a given date, and the additions of loan books to stock during the year. Do the figures below support the idea that more additions to stock encourage more loans?

a) The figures may be used for more practice in calculating Pearson's correlation coefficient. For this sample, if $\alpha = 0.01$, the critical value of $r = 0.561$.

b) Use the figures to construct a regression line of Y (loans) on X (additions).

Additions during current year (000s)	Books on loan on 31 March (000s)
3	9
4	10
23	48
5	17

7	18
3	7
5	16
8	22
14	35
9	25
11	25
1	8
10	29
16	67
16	30
12	32
13	32
17	34
18	41
15	55
210	560

Conclusion

Now you have worked through this text, we hope that you feel inspired and confident to apply the ideas to the study and monitoring of your own library and information service. The examples given show something of the range of aspects of work that are amenable to statistical analysis, and your own ingenuity will suggest others. You will also be able to examine other people's statistical statements with an informed eye, and evaluate them more wisely.

Statistics is only a tool. It must always be remembered that statistics – particularly inferential statistics – never 'proves' anything. A conclusion is reached on the grounds of its probability only. Strong assertions should not be made solely on the strength of a statistical test. Many other factors may have to taken into account in explaining the phenomenon discussed. The average student use of the college library must recognize times when student use is minimal, as in vacations. In a test of association and correlation, we might find a high coincidence of antisocial behaviour and sales of a particular newspaper, but we would be incautious to regard that newspaper as a bad influence. There could be other social factors which influence people to buy that paper and commit antisocial acts.

Statistics is related to what is broadly called 'research methods'. This is another story (and another book) but enough has been said in this present text to show that results can be no better than the data on which they are based. Data should be collected with a view to what you intend to do with them. For certain types of calculation data must be recorded on the interval/ratio scale, for instance. The need to avoid bias has been noted. Research methods teachers will discuss questionnaire design. It is remarkably difficult to design a questionnaire whose questions will be understood by the respondent as the designer meant them, and which will elicit answers with enough fulness and objectivity to be useful.

Computer software

We have reached this far without discussing computers, although their rudimentary strength as number-processing engines is well-known.

One statistical package is Minitab, a system easy to learn and use. It is available for PCs and minicomputers. SPSS (Statistical Package for the Social Sciences) requires a little more effort to learn, but offers a sophisticated range of analyses; this also has a PC version. Some programs are written for particular computers, such as the 'First' family of multi-tasking suites written for use on Acorn Risc machines.

Spreadsheets like QuattroPro and Lotus 1-2-3, besides tabulation of numerical data, permit arithmetical and statistical operations on figures. Recent versions of Minitab provide a spreadsheet mode as an alternative to working in columns.

Automated library management systems have been mentioned elsewhere, as sources of an abundance of raw data and possible analysis.

Graphics facilities are included in most packages, some better than others, but allowing production of graphs as well as other forms of data presentation.

Without going into detail, we can note that there is a good choice of software available for the information profession for use on general personal computers, which will take away a lot of the drudgery of performing the statistical processes described in this text, and more besides. Some of them were in fact written to aid in the teaching of statistics, and are accessible and friendly to use. It is necessary for the user to understand the processes which the programs perform so efficiently. The programs don't give the results a greater validity than the input deserves, and the interpretation and evaluation are still the burden of the researcher.

Appendix 1
Answers to practice questions

Chapter 2 Elements of statistics

1   Age of students – V; voting age – C; scores obtained – V; score obtainable – C; public transport – V; shares – V (C if a given year).
2   In Study A, intelligence is the independent variable.
     In Study B, intelligence is the dependent variable.
3   [1] population; [2] sample; [3] independent variable; [4] case; [5] frequency; [6] value of dependent variable; [7] independent variable.
4   sex, colour, occupation, religious persuasion.
5   fluoride – I/R; insects – N; reaction time – I/R; graded question – O; league position – O; hamsters – I/R; class – O; hardness – O.
6   hair – C; disruptions – D; acquisitions – D; anxiety – C; intelligence – C; reading ability – C; space – C; doctors – D.

Maths refresher

1) 37	10) –4	18) 66.6%, 273%
2) 16	11) 36	19) 22.5%
3) 10	12) –970	20) 37.73%
4) –196	13) –7	21) 47.5p
5) 196	14) impossible	22) 83/100
6) 1	15) 1 (any value raised	23) 117.2
7) –10 (or 25)	to power 0 = 1)	24) 2696.143
8) 15	16) 1	25) 3.3
9) 25	17) 32	26) 0.2109

Chapter 3 Percentages, proportions and ratios

1.1 Commuting in/out. Not possible to say where everybody is going.
1.2 They are estimates to the nearest 1000
1.3 Figures show per 1000 population. Makes figures more comparable. Metropolis may be weighted, balance of staff grades? Length of time in post?

1.4 Salaries per 1000 population $\times \dfrac{\text{resident population}}{1\,000}$

$= £6964 \times \dfrac{127\,700}{1\,000} = £889\,302$

£889,302

1.5

	City	%	Newtown	%
Professionals	0.304	30.43	0.3	30.13
Non-Professionals	0.5	50	0.6	59.8
Manual	0.196	19.57	0.1	10.04
Totals	1	100	1	99.97

It would be reasonable to apply rounding to Newtown's percentages, as has been done with the proportions.

1.6 City   1:1.388
    Newtown   1:1.195
1.7 Newtown has more staff per 1000 than City.
1.8

	City	Newtown
Reference	11.87%	8.54%
Fiction	30.58	22.6
Non-fiction	38.23	49.56
Children's	19.32	19.3

Chapter 4 Organizing data

1

	f	%		f	%
15–19	3	6%	15–24	5	10%
20–24	2	4	25–34	13	26
25–29	7	14	35–44	15	30
30–34	6	12	45–54	12	24
35–39	7	14	55–64	5	10
40–44	8	16		$n = 50$	
45–49	6	12			
50–54	6	12			
55–59	3	6			
60–64	2	4			
	$n = 50$				

2   Model graphs are not given. You should check your own for proportions, labelling, clear keys, clarity, scaling.

Chapter 5 Measures of central tendency

1   Raw data: mean = 17.49, median = 18, mode = 20
    Grouped data: mean = 17.9, median = 14.36, modal class 16–20

Chapter 6 Measures of dispersion

1

Age	f	%		cum%
			<15	0
15–19	3	6%	<20	6
20–24	2	4	<25	10
25–29	7	14	<30	24
30–34	6	12	<35	36
35–39	7	14	<40	50
40–44	8	16	<45	66
45–49	6	12	<50	78
50–54	6	12	<55	90
55–59	3	6	<60	96
60–64	2	4	<65	100

$N = 50$

The ogive correctly constructed should give an IQR of c.21. This is calculated making allowances for inaccuracy and imprecision in hand drawing the ogive.

2

	x	f	fx	$(x - \bar{x})$	$(x - \bar{x})^2$	$(x - \bar{x})^2 f$
0–4	2	5	10	−7.8	60.84	304.2
5–9	7	19	133	−2.8	7.84	148.96
10–14	12	19	228	2.2	2.84	91.96
15–19	17	7	119	7.2	51.84	362.88
		50	490			908

Mean = 490/50 = 9.8
sd = $\sqrt{908/49}$ = 4.3

Chapter 7 Time series, index numbers

$$I = \frac{\Sigma P_N Q_O}{\Sigma P_O Q_O} \times 100$$

$$I = \frac{(45 \times 253) + (30 \times 124) + (17 \times 54)}{(35 \times 253) + (20 \times 124) + (12 \times 54)}$$

$$I = \frac{16\,023}{11\,983}$$

$$I = 133.7$$

Chapter 8 Introducing inferential statistics and probability

1   5/8
2   a) and c)
3   $3/14 \times 3/10 \times 2/15 \times 4/10 = 72/53760 = 0.00134$
4   Strictly, the probability is
    $50/1000 \times 49/999 \times 48/998 = 0.0001179$

Chapter 9 Binomial distribution

1 a) $p(0) = \begin{pmatrix} 10 \\ 0 \end{pmatrix} \times (0.32)^0 \times (0.68)^{10}$

   $= 1 \times 1 \times 0.021$, so
   $p(0) = 0.021$

   b) $p(7) = \begin{pmatrix} 10 \\ 7 \end{pmatrix} \times (0.32)^7 \times (0.68)^3$

   $= 120 \times (0.32)^7 \times (0.68)^3 = 0.01296$

   c) p(more than 2) means $p(3) + p(4) \ldots + p(10)$, calculating all their probabilities
   and adding them together. A quicker way is to calculate $p(0)$, $p(1)$, and $p(2)$,
   add their probabilities together, subtract the total from 1.
   $p(0)$ we already have.

   $p(1) = \begin{pmatrix} 10 \\ 1 \end{pmatrix} = 10 \times (0.32)^1 \times (0.68)^9 = 0.0995$

   $p(2) = \begin{pmatrix} 10 \\ 2 \end{pmatrix} = 45 \times (0.32)^2 \times (0.68)^8 = 0.2107$

   $p(0 + 1 + 2) = 0.021 + 0.0995 + 0.2107 = 0.3312$

   p(more than two) $= 1 - 0.3312 = 0.6688$

2 a) The observed proportion of books found was
   $$\frac{7241}{9821} = 0.737,$$
   so 0.737 can be taken as the probability that any desired book will be found
   without assistance. The strategy for solving this problem is similar to the
   previous one.

   b) i $= 0.118$
   ii $p(0) + p(1) + p(2)$. added, subtracted from 1.
   $p(0) = 0.000087$, $p(1) = 0.0017$, $p(2) = 0.014$, total $= 0.016$. So p(at least
   two) $= 1 - 0.016 = 0.984$

3   Music Library
   $p(10) = 0.277$, $p(11) = 0.337$, $p(12) = 0.188$
   p(at least 10) $= 0.802$

Chapter 11 Inference from sample to population

1   $95\%CI = 9.8 \pm (1.96 \times \dfrac{4.3}{\sqrt{50}}) = 9.8 \pm 1.19$

$= 8.61 < \mu < 10.99$ hours

2   $99\%CI = 35.9 \pm (2.575 \times \dfrac{21.85}{\sqrt{75}})$

$= 29.4 < \mu < 42.397$

As claims are a discrete variable the fractions are meaningless, so round up or down as appropriate, giving
$29 < \mu < 42$

3   $n = 25$, df $= 24$, t.025 $= 2.064$

$95\% \text{ CI} = 13 \pm (2.064 \times \dfrac{1.8}{\sqrt{25}}) = 13 \pm 0.743$

$= 12.257 < \mu < 13.743$ rounded (as visitors are a discrete variable) to $12 < \mu < 14$

Chapter 12 Introduction to hypothesis testing

1   Set out the test parameters:

$H_0 : \mu = 70$ copies	sample statistics
$H_1 : \mu < 70$	$n = 40$
$\alpha = 0.01$, so $CV_z = -2.33$	$\bar{x} = 66$
	$s = 7$

The test: $z = \dfrac{66 - 70}{\dfrac{7}{\sqrt{40}}} = -3.6$

The difference is greater than the critical value, so it is accepted that it is greater than can be explained by chance. The decision, at the 99% level of confidence, is to reject the null hypothesis: the machine is uneconomical.

2   H_1 could be that $\mu \neq 130$ or that $\mu < 130$. The test statistic is that $z = -1.18$, so by either test the statistic is less than the critical value. At this level of confidence, then, the null hypothesis can be retained.

3   Take $H_0 : \mu = 37.5$ years (the national average)
and $H_1 : \mu = 37.5$ years (Blackbury's average is different)
The test statistic z is 5.925, well beyond the critical value of 1.96, so at the 95% level of confidence the null hypothesis is rejected, i.e. Blackbury central library users are older than the average in the national survey.

Chapter 13 Two-means tests

1. $H_0 : \mu_1 = \mu_2 \quad H_1 : \mu_1 \neq \mu_2 \quad \alpha = 0.05 \quad CV_z = 1.96$

$$z = \frac{20.1 - 18.3}{\sqrt{\dfrac{12.96}{52} + \dfrac{7.84}{33}}} = 2.5798$$

There is a significant difference at the chosen level of confidence. Had $\alpha = 0.01$, the critical value would have been 2.575. The test statistic exceeds that, but only very marginally.

2. Since the argument is that Branch Z is thought to be busier, frame the test so that Branch X is less than Branch Z
i.e. that $H_1 : \mu_1 < \mu_2$. With $\alpha = 0.05$, $CV_z = -1.645$
z calculates at −1.849, which is beyond the limit containing 95% of the differences, so the difference cannot be attributed to chance. The librarian can conclude, therefore, that the difference is significant, and that Branch Z does issue more.

3. The interest is clearly in showing that the new procedure is faster, so identify groups accordingly, to give the alternate hypothesis that μ_1 (old) is $< \mu_2$ (new).
$CV_z = -1.645$
Sample z calculates as −2.05, so the difference is significant at 0.05, the new procedure is accepted as faster than the old.

Chapter 14 Proportions

1. The tactic would be to take the desired target of 75% as the null hypothesis, and see whether the sample supports this or falls significantly short of it.
$H_0 : \Pi = 0.75$
$H_1 : \Pi < 0.75 \qquad P_s = 83/120 = 0.69$
$\alpha = 0.01$, so $CV_z = -2.33$

$$z = \frac{0.69 - 0.75}{\sqrt{\dfrac{0.75 \times 0.25}{120}}} = 1.5178$$

Calculated z is well within the critical value. The difference is deemed to be by chance, and the target figure is supported by the sample. Although 69% is less than 75% it is not significantly less, at this level of confidence.

2. Taking the view that the true proportion is not equal to 0.35, critical value of z is 2.575, the test calculates as −1.258. The difference is within the limits of chance, so the null hypothesis is retained.

3   With the alternative hypothesis that $\Pi_1 = \Pi_2$, $CV_z = 1.96$
$p_s1 = 19/50 = 0.38$ $p_s2 = 12/40 = 0.3$
$$p_p = \frac{19 + 12}{50 + 40} = 0.34$$

$$\text{test } z = \frac{0.38 - 0.3}{\sqrt{\dfrac{0.34(0.66)}{50} + \dfrac{0.34(0.66)}{40}}} = 0.796$$

The difference is less than the critical value, i.e. it is within the limit of difference by chance only, so the difference between the two readerships is not significant.

4   Taking it that $\Pi_1 = \Pi_2$, the critical value of z is 1.96.
Sample proportion 1 is 0.08, sample proportion 2 is 0.05, pooled proportion is 0.06. The test difference calculates as $z = 1.458$, so the difference is not significant at the chosen level of confidence.

Chapter 15 Bivariate statistics

1   a) Course 1 proportion of absentees is $26/94 = 0.277$. Course 2 $= 65/185 = 0.35$, Course 3 $= 77/292 = 0.26$

b)

	Absent	Not	
Course 1	26	68	94
	27.66	66.34	
Course 2	65	120	185
	54.43	130.57	
Course 3	77	215	292
	85.91	206.09	
	168	403	571

H_0 : no association of course and absenteeism, therefore no difference in incidence of absenteeism
H_1 : there is a difference; Course 2 has a worse record.
$\alpha = 0.05$, degrees of freedom $= 2$, so $CV\chi^2 = 5.991$.

$O - E$	$(O - E)^2$	$(O - E)^2/E$
−1.66	2.7556	0.0996
10.57	111.7249	2.0526
−8.91	79.3881	0.9241
1.66	2.7556	0.0415
−10.57	111.7249	0.8557
8.91	79.3881	0.3852
		4.3587

which is χ^2 for the sample. As this is less than the critical value, the differences are held to be only due to chance, and do not indicate a significant difference between courses.

2   For this test $\alpha = 0.01$, df = 6, and $CV\chi^2$ is 16.812.

Sample χ^2 calculates as 19.94. Beyond the critical value, it is regarded as too large a value to have arisen by chance. The difference is therefore statistically significant, and we can believe that some students are more successful than others with catalogues.

3   If total absences are equalized over the days of the week, the librarian's figures look like this:

M	T	W	Th	F	
302	285	255	267	298	total 1407
281.4	281.4	281.4	281.4	281.4	

Degrees of freedom = 4, so $CV\chi^2 = 9.488$, when $\alpha = 0.05$.

The test calculates as 5.7467. This being less than the critical value, the differences are held to be not significant.

Chapter 16 Correlation and regression

1   Taking nursing staff as the x variable, and clerical staff as y:

x	y	$x - \bar{x}$	$(x - \bar{x})^2$	$y - \bar{y}$	$(y - \bar{y})^2$	$(x - x)(y - y)$
63	62	1	1	23	529	23
38	30	−24	576	−9	81	216
52	41	−10	100	2	4	−20
58	31	−4	16	−8	64	32
88	48	26	676	9	81	234
85	42	23	529	3	9	69
37	20	−25	625	−19	361	475
62	38	0	0	−1	1	0
93	50	31	961	11	121	341
44	28	−18	324	−11	121	198
			3808		1372	1568

$\bar{x} = 62$ $\bar{y} = 39$

substitute into the formula:

$$\frac{1568}{\sqrt{3808 \times 1372}} = 0.686$$

This is a 'fairly strong' correlation. As it exceeds the critical value of r, which shows the largest apparent correlation that could have arisen by sampling chance, it is deemed significant. We can conclude, therefore, that in general clerical staffs do rise with nursing staffs.

2   Take issues as independent variable x, and queries as dependent variable y.

x	x rank	y	y rank	d	d^2
41	8	43	9	−1	1
37.5	6	36	5.5	0.5	0.25
50.5	11	48	11	0	0
46	10	44	10	0	0
35.5	5	31	4	1	1
40.3	7	42	8	−1	1
42.1	9	38	7	2	4
27.9	2	30	3	−1	1
18.6	1	21	1	0	0
33.7	4	36	5.5	−1.5	2.25
53.4	12	51	12	0	0
30.7	3	24	2	1	1
					11.5

Entering figures into the formula,

$$r_s = 1 - \frac{6 \times 11.5}{12 \times 143} = 0.959 \; (0.96)$$

Test the significance of this coefficient:

$$t = 0.96 \sqrt{\frac{10}{1 - 0.9216}}$$

This equals 10.84, which is beyond the critical value of $t = 3.169$. The correlation is significant, and issues are a good indicator of a library's performance.

3   a) As a Pearson's correlation test, r for the sample $= 0.85$, a strong positive correlation. As it is beyond the critical value of 0.561, the limit of apparent correlation by chance, the correlation is deemed to be significant.

   b) As a regression analysis, take 'additions' a the independent variable x, and 'books on loan' as the dependent variable y.

x	y	x^2	xy
3	9	9	27
4	10	16	40
23	48	529	1104
5	17	25	85
7	18	49	126
3	7	9	21
5	16	25	80
8	22	64	176
14	35	196	490
9	25	81	225
11	25	121	275
1	8	1	8
10	29	100	290
16	67	256	1072
16	30	256	480
12	32	144	384
13	32	169	416
17	34	289	578
18	41	324	738
15	55	225	825
210	560	2888	7440

Put these figures into the normal equations:

1    $560 = 20a + 210b$
2    $7440 = 210a + 2888b$

To equalize the *a* values, multiply line 2 by 1, and line 1 by 10.5:

1    $5880 = 210a + 2205b$
2    $7440 = 210a + 2888b$

Cancel the *a* in each line, and subtract 1 from 2:

$1560 = 683b$

$\dfrac{1560}{683} = b$

$2.28 = b$

Substitute for *b* in 1:

$560 = 20a + 210\,(2.28)$
$560 = 20a + 478.8$
$560 - 478.8 = 20a$

$81.2 = 20a$

$4.06 = a$

These values of a and b can now be used in the formula $y' = a + b(x)$ for a high and a low value of x, and the regression line can be drawn on a graph.

Appendix 2
Statistical tables and formulae

Areas under the normal curve
Z-table

Z	0.00	0.01	0.02	0.03	0.04	0.05	0.06	0.07	0.08	0.09
-3.4	0.0003	0.0003	0.0003	0.0003	0.0003	0.0003	0.0003	0.0003	0.0003	0.0002
-3.3	0.0005	0.0005	0.0005	0.0004	0.0004	0.0004	0.0004	0.0004	0.0004	0.0003
-3.2	0.0007	0.0007	0.0006	0.0006	0.0006	0.0006	0.0006	0.0005	0.0005	0.0005
-3.1	0.0010	0.0009	0.0009	0.0009	0.0008	0.0008	0.0008	0.0008	0.0007	0.0007
-3.0	0.0013	0.0013	0.0013	0.0012	0.0012	0.0011	0.0011	0.0011	0.0010	0.0010
-2.9	0.0019	0.0018	0.0017	0.0017	0.0016	0.0016	0.0015	0.0015	0.0014	0.0014
-2.8	0.0026	0.0025	0.0024	0.0023	0.0023	0.0022	0.0021	0.0021	0.0020	0.0019
-2.7	0.0035	0.0034	0.0033	0.0032	0.0031	0.0030	0.0029	0.0028	0.0027	0.0026
-2.6	0.0047	0.0045	0.0044	0.0043	0.0041	0.0040	0.0039	0.0038	0.0037	0.0036
-2.5	0.0062	0.0060	0.0059	0.0057	0.0055	0.0054	0.0052	0.0051	0.0049	0.0048
-2.4	0.0082	0.0080	0.0078	0.0075	0.0073	0.0071	0.0069	0.0068	0.0066	0.0064
-2.3	0.0107	0.0104	0.0102	0.0099	0.0096	0.0094	0.0091	0.0089	0.0087	0.0084
-2.2	0.0139	0.0136	0.0132	0.0129	0.0125	0.0122	0.0119	0.0116	0.0113	0.0110
-2.1	0.0179	0.0174	0.0170	0.0166	0.0162	0.0158	0.0154	0.0150	0.0146	0.0143
-2.0	0.0228	0.0222	0.0217	0.0212	0.0207	0.0202	0.0197	0.0192	0.0188	0.0183
-1.9	0.0287	0.0281	0.0274	0.0268	0.0262	0.0256	0.0250	0.0244	0.0239	0.0233
-1.8	0.0359	0.0352	0.0344	0.0336	0.0329	0.0322	0.0314	0.0307	0.0301	0.0294
-1.7	0.0446	0.0436	0.0427	0.0418	0.0409	0.0401	0.0392	0.0384	0.0375	0.0367
-1.6	0.0548	0.0537	0.0526	0.0516	0.0505	0.0495	0.0485	0.0475	0.0465	0.0455
-1.5	0.0668	0.0655	0.0643	0.0630	0.0618	0.0606	0.0594	0.0582	0.0571	0.0559
-1.4	0.0808	0.0793	0.0778	0.0764	0.0749	0.0735	0.0722	0.0708	0.0694	0.0681
-1.3	0.0968	0.0951	0.0934	0.0918	0.0901	0.0885	0.0869	0.0853	0.0838	0.0823
-1.2	0.1151	0.1131	0.1112	0.1093	0.1075	0.1056	0.1038	0.1020	0.1003	0.0985
-1.1	0.1357	0.1335	0.1314	0.1292	0.1271	0.1251	0.1230	0.1210	0.1190	0.1170
-1.0	0.1587	0.1562	0.1539	0.1515	0.1492	0.1469	0.1446	0.1423	0.1401	0.1379
-0.9	0.1841	0.1814	0.1788	0.1762	0.1736	0.1711	0.1685	0.1660	0.1635	0.1611
-0.8	0.2119	0.2090	0.2061	0.2033	0.2005	0.1977	0.1949	0.1922	0.1894	0.1867
-0.7	0.2420	0.2389	0.2358	0.2327	0.2296	0.2266	0.2236	0.2206	0.2177	0.2148
-0.6	0.2743	0.2709	0.2676	0.2643	0.2611	0.2578	0.2546	0.2514	0.2483	0.2451
-0.5	0.3085	0.3050	0.3015	0.2981	0.2946	0.2912	0.2877	0.2843	0.2810	0.2776
-0.4	0.3446	0.3409	0.3372	0.3336	0.3300	0.3264	0.3228	0.3192	0.3156	0.3121
-0.3	0.3821	0.3783	0.3745	0.3707	0.3669	0.3632	0.3594	0.3557	0.3520	0.3483
-0.2	0.4207	0.4168	0.4129	0.4090	0.4052	0.4013	0.3974	0.3936	0.3897	0.3859
-0.1	0.4602	0.4562	0.4522	0.4483	0.4443	0.4404	0.4364	0.4325	0.4286	0.4247
-0.0	0.5000	0.4960	0.4920	0.4880	0.4840	0.4801	0.4761	0.4721	0.4681	0.4641

0.0	0.5000	0.5040	0.5080	0.5120	0.5160	0.5199	0.5239	0.5279	0.5319	0.5359
0.1	0.5398	0.5438	0.5478	0.5517	0.5557	0.5596	0.5636	0.5675	0.5714	0.5753
0.2	0.5793	0.5832	0.5871	0.5910	0.5948	0.5987	0.6026	0.6064	0.6103	0.6141
0.3	0.6179	0.6217	0.6255	0.6293	0.6331	0.6368	0.6406	0.6443	0.6480	0.6517
0.4	0.6554	0.6591	0.6628	0.6664	0.6700	0.6736	0.6772	0.6808	0.6844	0.6879
0.5	0.6915	0.6950	0.6985	0.7019	0.7054	0.7088	0.7123	0.7157	0.7190	0.7224
0.6	0.7257	0.7291	0.7324	0.7357	0.7389	0.7422	0.7454	0.7486	0.7517	0.7549
0.7	0.7580	0.7611	0.7642	0.7673	0.7704	0.7734	0.7764	0.7794	0.7823	0.7852
0.8	0.7881	0.7910	0.7939	0.7967	0.7995	0.8023	0.8051	0.8078	0.8106	0.8133
0.9	0.8159	0.8186	0.8212	0.8238	0.8264	0.8289	0.8315	0 8340	0.8365	0.8389
1.0	0.8413	0.8438	0.8461	0.8485	0.8508	0.8531	0.8554	0.8577	0.8599	0.8621
1.1	0.8643	0.8665	0.8686	0.8708	0.8729	0.8749	0.8770	0.8790	0.8810	0.8830
1.2	0.8849	0.8869	0.8888	0.8907	0.8925	0.8944	0.8962	0.8980	0.8997	0.9015
1.3	0.9032	0.9049	0.9066	0.9082	0.9099	0.9115	0.9131	0.9147	0.9162	0.9177
1.4	0.9192	0.9207	0.9222	0.9236	0.9251	0.9265	0.9278	0.9292	0.9306	0.9319
1.5	0.9332	0.9345	0.9357	0.9370	0.9382	0.9394	0.9406	0.9418	0.9429	0.9441
1.6	0.9452	0.9463	0.9474	0.9484	0.9495	0.9505	0.9515	0.9525	0.9535	0.9545
1.7	0.9554	0.9564	0.9573	0.9582	0.9591	0.9599	0.9608	0.9616	0.9625	0.9633
1.8	0.9641	0.9649	0.9656	0.9664	0.9671	0.9678	0.9686	0.9693	0.9699	0.9706
1.9	0.9713	0.9719	0.9726	0.9732	0.9738	0.9744	0.9750	0.9756	0.9761	0.9767
2.0	0.9772	0.9778	0.9783	0.9788	0.9793	0.9798	0.9803	0.9808	0.9812	0.9817
2.1	0.9821	0.9826	0.9830	0.9834	0.9838	0.9842	0.9846	0.9850	0.9854	0.9857
2.2	0.9861	0.9864	0.9868	0.9871	0.9875	0.9878	0.9881	0.9884	0.9887	0.9890
2.3	0.9893	0.9896	0.9898	0.9901	0.9904	0.9906	0.9909	0.9911	0.9913	0.9916
2.4	0.9918	0.9920	0.9922	0.9925	0.9927	0.9929	0.9931	0.9932	0.9934	0.9936
2.5	0.9938	0.9940	0.9941	0.9943	0.9945	0.9946	0.9948	0.9949	0.9951	0.9952
2.6	0.9953	0.9955	0.9956	0.9957	0.9959	0.9960	0.9961	0.9962	0.9963	0.9964
2.7	0.9965	0.9966	0.9967	0.9968	0.9969	0.9970	0.9971	0.9972	0.9973	0.9974
2.8	0.9974	0.9975	0.9976	0.9977	0.9977	0.9978	0.9979	0.9979	0.9980	0.9981
2.9	0.9981	0.9982	0.9982	0.9983	0.9984	0.9984	0.9985	0.9985	0.9986	0.9986
3.0	0.9987	0.9987	0.9987	0.9988	0.9988	0.9989	0.9989	0.9989	0.9990	0.9990
3.1	0.9990	0.9991	0.9991	0.9991	0.9992	0.9992	0.9992	0.9992	0.9993	0.9993
3.2	0.9993	0.9993	0.9994	0.9994	0.9994	0.9994	0.9994	0.9995	0.9995	0.9995
3.3	0.9995	0.9995	0.9995	0.9996	0.9996	0.9996	0.9996	0.9996	0.9996	0.9997
3.4	0.9997	0.9997	9.9997	0.9997	0.9997	0.9997	0.9997	0.9997	0.9997	0.9998

Table of the *t*-distribution

df	t.050	t.025	t.01	t.005	df
1	6.314	12.706	31.821	63.657	1
2	2.920	4.303	6.965	9.925	2
3	2.353	3.182	4.541	5.841	3
4	2.132	2.776	3.747	4.604	4
5	2.015	2.571	3.365	4.032	5
6	1.943	2.447	3.143	3.707	6
7	1.895	2.365	2.998	3.499	7
8	1.860	2.306	2.896	3.355	8
9	1.833	2.262	2.821	3.250	9
10	1.812	2.228	2.764	3.169	10
11	1.796	2.201	2.718	3.106	11
12	1.782	2.179	2.681	3.055	12
13	1.771	2.160	2.650	3.012	13
14	1.761	2.145	2.624	2.977	14
15	1.753	2.131	2.602	2.947	15
16	1.746	2.120	2.583	2.921	16
17	1.740	2.110	2.567	2.898	17
18	1.734	2.101	2.552	2.878	18
19	1.729	2.093	2.539	2.861	19
20	1.725	2.086	2.528	2.845	20
21	1.721	2.080	2.518	2.831	21
22	1.717	2.074	2.508	2.819	22
23	1.714	2.069	2.500	2.807	23
24	1.711	2.064	2.492	2.797	24
25	1.708	2.060	2.485	2.787	25
26	1.706	2.056	2.479	2.779	26
27	1.703	2.052	2.473	2.771	27
28	1.701	2.048	2.467	2.763	28
29	1.699	2.045	2.462	2.756	29
inf	1.645	1.960	2.326	2.576	30

Reproduced with permission from Hayslett, H. T., *Statistics made simple*, 3rd edn., Heinemann, 1985.

Table of the χ^2 distribution

df	χ^2 .05	χ^2 .01	df
1	3.841	6.635	1
2	5.991	9.210	2
3	7.815	11.345	3
4	9.488	13.277	4
5	11.070	15.086	5
6	12.592	16.812	6
7	14.067	18.475	7
8	15.507	20.090	8
9	16.919	21.666	9
10	18.307	23.209	10
11	19.675	24.725	11
12	21.026	26.217	12
13	22.362	27.688	13
14	23.685	29.141	14
15	24.996	30.578	15
16	26.296	32.000	16
17	27.587	33.409	17
18	28.869	34.805	18
19	30.144	36.191	19
20	31.410	37.566	20
21	32.671	38.932	21
22	33.924	40.289	22
23	35.172	41.638	23
24	36.415	42.980	24
25	37.652	44.314	25
26	38.885	45.642	26
27	40.113	46.963	27
28	41.337	48.278	28
29	42.557	49.588	29
30	43.773	50.892	30

Reproduced with permission from Elifsen, K., *Fundamentals of social statistics*, 2nd edn., McGraw-Hill, 1990.

Statistical formulae
The arithmetic mean

a) for single data

$$\bar{x} = \frac{\Sigma x}{n}$$

b) with frequencies

$$\bar{x} = \frac{\Sigma f.x}{\Sigma f}$$

c) grouped data

$$\bar{x} = \frac{\Sigma f.\acute{x}}{\Sigma f}$$

where $\acute{x}$ = the class midpoints

The standard deviation of a sample

$$s = \sqrt{\frac{\Sigma (x - \bar{x})^2}{n - 1}}$$

Or, for a frequency distribution,

$$s = \sqrt{\frac{\Sigma (x - \bar{x})^2 \times f}{\Sigma f - 1}}$$

Permutations

$_nP_r$ (the number of permutations of r objects taken from a set of n objects)

$$= \frac{n!}{(n - r)!}$$

Combinations

$_nC_r$ (the number of combinations of n objects taken r at a time)

$$= \binom{n}{r} = \frac{n!}{r! \times (n - r)!}$$

Binomial probabilities

$p(r)$ = the probability of r successes in n independent trials

$$= \binom{n}{r} \times p^r \times (1 - p)^{n-r}$$

Standard units

for a sample:
$$z = \frac{x - \bar{x}}{s}$$

for a population:
$$z = \frac{X - \mu}{\sigma}$$

Confidence intervals for a sample mean

for a large sample:
$$CI = \bar{x} \pm \left(z \times \frac{s}{\sqrt{n}}\right)$$

for a small sample:
$$CI = \bar{x} \pm \left(t \times \frac{s}{\sqrt{n}}\right)$$

Standard error of the sampling distribution of means

$$SE = \frac{s}{\sqrt{n}} \quad \text{i.e.} \quad \frac{\text{the standard deviation of the sample}}{\text{the square root of } n \text{ in the sample}}$$

Test statistic for the significance of a single mean

$$z = \frac{\bar{x} - \mu_0}{\frac{s}{\sqrt{n}}}$$

Standard error of the sampling distribution of differences between means

$$\sigma_{(\bar{x}_1 - \bar{x}_2)} = \sqrt{\frac{s_1^2}{n_1} + \frac{s_2^2}{n_2}}$$

Test statistic for the difference between two means (large samples)

$$z = \frac{\bar{x}_1 - \bar{x}_2}{\sqrt{\frac{s_1^2}{n_1} + \frac{s_2^2}{n_2}}}$$

Confidence interval for a proportion

$$CI_\Pi = p_s \pm (z \times \sqrt{\frac{p_s(1 - p_s)}{n}})$$

Significance test for a proportion (large samples)

$$z = \frac{p_s - p_0}{\sqrt{\frac{p_0(1 - p_0)}{n}}}$$

Significance test for the difference between two proportions (large samples)

1. pooled proportion: $\quad p_p = \dfrac{x_1 + x_2}{n_1 + n_2}$

2. test statistic: $\quad z = \dfrac{p_{s_1} - p_{s_2}}{\sqrt{\dfrac{p_p(1 - p_p)}{n_1} + \dfrac{p_p(1 - p_p)}{n_2}}}$

Chi-square (χ^2) test of independence

$$\chi^2 = \sum \frac{(O - E)^2}{E}$$

Pearson's produce-moment coefficient of correlation (Pearson's r)

$$r = \frac{\Sigma(x - \bar{x})(y - \bar{y})}{\sqrt{\Sigma(x - \bar{x})^2 \times \Sigma(y - \bar{y})^2}}$$

Standard error of r

$$SE_r = \frac{1 - (r)^2}{\sqrt{n}}$$

Spearman's rank correlation coefficient (r_s)

$$r_s = 1 - (\frac{6 \times \Sigma d^2}{n(n^2 - 1)})$$

Test statistics for a Spearman-derived coefficient

1. large sample:

$$z = r_s\sqrt{n - 1}$$

2. small sample:

$$t = r_s\sqrt{\frac{n - 2}{1 - r_s^2}}$$

Regression

$$y = a + b.x$$

The normal equations

(1) $\Sigma y = na + b(\Sigma x)$
(2) $\Sigma xy = a(\Sigma x) + b(\Sigma x^2)$

Appendix 3
Bibliography

Blalock, H. M., *Social statistics,* Rev. 2nd edn., McGraw-Hill, 1979.

Chapman, M., *Plain figures,* London, HMSO, 1986.

Clark, P., *Using statistics in business*, Pan, 1982.

Clegge, F., *Simple statistics: a course book*, CUP, 1982.

Devore, J., *Introductory statistics*, West, 1990.

Fletcher, J. P., *How to write a report*, IPM, 1983.

Freund, J. E., *Statistics: a first course,* 5th edn., Prentice-Hall, 1991. (3rd and 4th eds. are still useful).

Graham. A., *Investigating statistics: a beginner's guide*, Hodder & Stoughton, 1990.

Hamburg, M., *Basic statistics*, HBJ, 1985.

Harper, W. M., *Statistics*, 6th edn., London, Macdonald & Evans, 1991. (Earlier editions also useful).

Jaeger, R. M., *Statistics: a spectator sport*, 2nd edn., Newburn Park, Ca., Sage, 1990. (This explains the reasoning behind statistical processes, and is a useful complement to the how-to-do-it type of text).

Kennedy, G., *Invitation to statistics*, Robertson, 1983.

Loether, H. J. and McTavish, D. G., *Descriptive statistics for sociologists*, Allyn & Bacon, 1974.

H. J. Loether and D. G. McTavish, *Inferential statistics for sociologists,* Allyn & Bacon, 1974.

Losee, R. M. and Worley, K. A., *Research and evaluation for information professionals*, Academic Press, 1993.

Moore, D. S., *Statistics: concepts and controversies*, 3rd edn., Freeman, 1991. (Like Jaeger's book, this is more concerned with understanding than with techniques).

Paulos, J.A., *Innumeracy: mathematical illiteracy and its consequences*, London, Penguin, 1988. (A short and excellent book for those who are 'no good at maths'. Worth buying.)

Rowntree, D., *Probability*, London, Edward Arnold, 1984.

Rowntree, D., *Statistics without tears: a primer for non-mathematicians*, London, Penguin, 1981. (Worth buying.)

Simpson, I. S., *Basic statistics for librarians*, 3rd edn., London, Library Association Publishing, 1988.

Simpson, I. S., *How to interpret statistical data: a guide for librarians and information scientists*, London, Library Association Publishing, 1990.

Tufte, E. R., *Visual display of quantitative information*, Graphics Press, 1983.

Van Emden, J. and Eastal, J., *Report writing*, McGraw-Hill, 1987.

Index